Bill Nye's
Comic History
of the United States

Bill Nye

Illustrated by F. Opper

DODO PRESS

Bill Nye's

HISTORY

OF THE

UNITED
STATES

ILLUSTRATED BY

F. Opper

PREFACE.

Facts in a nude state are not liable criminally, any more than bright and beautiful children commit a felony by being born thus; but it is the solemn duty of those having these children in charge to put appropriate, healthful, and even attractive apparel upon them at the earliest possible moment.

It is thus with facts. They are the frame-work of history, not the drapery. They are like the cold, hard, dishevelled, damp, and uncomfortable body under the knife of the demonstrator, not the bright and bounding boy, clothed in graceful garments and filled to every tingling capillary with a soul.

We, each of us, the artist and the author, respect facts. We have never, either of us, said an unkind word regarding facts. But we believe that they should not be placed before the public exactly as they were born. We want to see them embellished and beautified. That is why this history is written.

Certain facts have come into the possession of the artist and author of this book regarding the history of the Republic down to the present day. We find, upon looking over the records and documents on file in the various archives of state and nation, that they are absolutely beyond question, and it is our object to give these truthfully. These rough and untidy, but impregnable truths, dressed in the sweet persuasive language of the author, and fluted, embossed, embroidered, and embellished by the skilful hand of the artist, are now before you.

History is but the record of the public and official acts of human beings. It is our object, therefore, to humanize our history and deal with people past and present; people who ate and possibly drank; people who were born, flourished, and died; not grave tragedians, posing perpetually for their photographs.

If we succeed in this way, and administer historical truth in the smooth capsule of the cartoonist and the commentator, we are content. If not, we know whose fault it will be, but will not get mad and swear about it.

BILL NYE.

FRED'K B. OPPER.

CONTENTS

CHAPTER I.

THE DISCOVERY OF AMERICA.

It was a beautiful evening at the close of a warm, luscious day in old Spain. It was such an evening as one would select for trysting purposes. The honeysuckle gave out the sweet announcement of its arrival on the summer breeze, and the bulbul sang in the dark vistas of olive-trees,—sang of his love and his hope, and of the victory he anticipated in the morrow's bulbul-fight, and the plaudits of the royal couple who would be there. The pink west paled away to the touch of twilight, and the soft zenith was sown with stars coming like celestial fire-flies on the breast of a mighty meadow.

Across the dusk, with bowed head, came a woman. Her air was one of proud humility. It was the air of royalty in the presence of an overruling power. It was Isabella. She was on her way to confession.

She carried a large, beautifully-bound volume containing a memorandum of her sins for the day. Ever and anon she would refer to it, but the twilight had come on so fast that she could not read it.

ISABELLA AT CONFESSIONAL.

Reaching the confessional, she kneeled, and, by the aid of her notes, she told off to the good Father and receptacle of the queen's trifling sins, Fernando de Talavera, how wicked she had been. When it was over and the queen had risen to go, Fernando came forth, and with a solemn obeisance said, —

'May it please your Majesty, I have to-day received a letter from my good friend the prior of the Franciscan convent of St. Mary's of Rabida in Andalusia. With your Majesty's permission, I will read it to you.'

'Proceed,' exclaimed Isabella, gravely, taking a piece of crochet-work from her apron and seating herself comfortably near the dim light.

'It is dated the sixth month and tenth day of the month, and reads as follows:

'DEAR BROTHER:

'This letter will be conveyed unto your hands by the bearer hereof. His name is Christopher Columbus, a native of Genoa, who has been living on me for two years. But he is a good man, devout and honest. He is willing to work, but I have nothing to do in his line. Times, as you know, are dull, and in his own profession nothing seems to be doing.

'He is by profession a discoverer. He has been successful in the work where he has had opportunities, and there has been no complaint so far on the part of those who have employed him. Everything he has ever discovered has remained that way, so he is willing to let his work show for itself.

'Should you be able to bring this to the notice of her Majesty, who is tender of heart, I would be most glad; and should her most gracious Majesty have any discovering to be done, or should she contemplate a change or desire to substitute another in the place of the present discoverer, she will do well to consider the qualifications of my friend.

'Very sincerely and fraternally thine,
'Etc., etc.'

The queen inquired still further regarding Columbus, and, taking the letter, asked Talavera to send him to the royal sitting-room at ten o'clock the following day.

When Columbus arose the next morning he found a note from the royal confessor, and, without waiting for breakfast, for he had almost overcome the habit of eating, he reversed his cuffs, and, taking a fresh handkerchief from his valise and putting it in his pocket so that the corners would coyly stick out a little, he was soon on his way to the palace. He carried also a small globe wrapped up in a newspaper.

The interview was encouraging until the matter of money necessary for the trip was touched upon. His Majesty was called in, and spoke sadly of the public surplus. He said that there were one hundred dollars still due on his own salary, and the palace had not been painted for eight years. He had taken orders on the store till he was tired of it. 'Our meat bill,' said he, taking off his crown and mashing a hornet on the wall, 'is sixty days overdue. We owe the hired girl for three weeks; and how are we going to get funds enough to do any discovering, when you remember that we have got to pay for an extra session this fall for the purpose of making money plenty?'

COLUMBUS AT COURT.

But Isabella came and sat by him in her winning way, and with the moistened corner of her handkerchief removed a spot of maple syrup from the ermine trimming of his reigning gown. She patted his hand, and, with her gentle voice, cheered him and told him that if he would economize and go without cigars or wine, in less than two hundred years he would have saved enough to fit Columbus out.

A few weeks later he had saved one hundred and fifty dollars in this way. The queen then went at twilight and pawned a large breastpin, and, although her chest was very sensitive to cold, she went without it all the following winter, in order that Columbus might discover America before immigration set in here.

Too much cannot be said of the heroism of Queen Isabella and the courage of her convictions. A man would have said, under such circumstances, that there would be no sense in discovering a place that was not popular. Why discover a place when it is so far out of the way? Why discover a country with no improvements? Why discover a country that is so far from the railroad? Why discover, at great expense, an entirely new country?

But Isabella did not stop to listen to these croaks. In the language of the Honorable Jeremiah M. Rusk, 'She seen her duty and she done it.' That was Isabella's style.

Columbus now began to select steamer-chairs and rugs. He had already secured the Niña, Pinta, and Santa Maria, and on the 3d of August, 1492, he sailed from Palos.

Isabella brought him a large bunch of beautiful flowers as he was about to sail, and Ferdinand gave him a nice yachting-cap and a spicy French novel to read on the road.

He was given a commission as viceroy or governor of all the lands he might discover, with hunting and shooting privileges on same.

COLUMBUS'S STEAMER-CHAIR.

He stopped several weeks at the Canary Islands, where he and his one hundred and twenty men rested and got fresh water. He then set out sailing due west over an unknown sea to blaze the way for liberty.

Soon, however, his men began to murmur. They began also to pick on Columbus and occupy his steamer-chair when he wanted to use it himself. They got to making chalk-marks on the deck and compelling him to pay a shilling before he could cross them. Some claimed that they were lost and that they had been sailing around for over a week in a circle, one man stating that he recognized a spot in the sea that they had passed eight times already.

Finally they mutinied, and started to throw the great navigator overboard, but he told them that if they would wait until the next morning he would tell them a highly amusing story that he heard just before he left Palos.

Thus his life was saved, for early in the morning the cry of 'Land ho!' was heard, and America was discovered.

A saloon was at once started, and the first step thus taken towards the foundation of a republic. From that one little timid saloon, with its family entrance, has sprung the magnificent and majestic machine which, lubricated with spoils and driven by wind, gives to every American to-day the right to live under a Government selected for him by men who make that their business.

Columbus discovered America several times after the 12th of October, 1492, and finally, while prowling about looking for more islands, discovered South America near the mouth of the Orinoco.

He was succeeded as governor by Francisco de Bobadilla, who sent him back finally in chains. Thus we see that the great are not always happy. There is no doubt that millions of people every year avoid many discomforts by remaining in obscurity.

COLUMBUS HAVING TROUBLE WITH HIS SAILORS.

The life of Columbus has been written by hundreds of men, both in this country and abroad, but the foregoing facts are distilled from this great biographical mass by skilful hands, and, like the succeeding pages, will stand for centuries unshaken by the bombardment of the critic, while succeeding years shall try them with frost and thaw, and the tide of time dash high against their massive front, only to recede, quelled and defeated.[1]

CHAPTER II.

OTHER DISCOVERIES—WET AND DRY.

America had many other discoverers besides Columbus, but he seems to have made more satisfactory arrangements with the historians than any of the others. He had genius, and was also a married man. He was a good after-dinner speaker, and was first to use the egg trick, which so many after-dinner speakers have since wished they had thought of before Chris did.

8

In falsifying the log-book in order to make his sailors believe that they had not sailed so far as they had, Columbus did a wrong act, unworthy of his high notions regarding the pious discovery of this land. The artist has shown here not only one of the most faithful portraits of Columbus and his crooked log-book, but the punishment which he should have received.

The man on the left is Columbus; History is concealed just around the corner in a loose wrapper.

Spain at this time regarded the new land as a vast jewelry store in charge of simple children of the forest who did not know the value of their rich agricultural lands or gold-ribbed farms. Spain, therefore, expected to exchange bone collar-buttons with the children of the forest for opals as large as lima beans, and to trade fiery liquids to them for large gold bricks.

The Montezumas were compelled every little while to pay a freight-bill for the Spanish confidence man.

Ponce de Leon had started out in search of the Hot Springs of Arkansas, and in 1512 came in sight of Florida. He was not successful in his attempt to find the Fountain of Youth, and returned an old man so deaf that in the language of the Hoosier poet referring to his grandfather, —

> 'So remarkably deaf was my grandfather Squeers
> That he had to wear lightning-rods over his ears
> To even hear thunder, and oftentimes then
> He was forced to request it to thunder again.'

Balboa crossed the Isthmus of Darien, and, rolling up his pantalettes, waded into the Pacific Ocean and discovered it in the name of Spain. It was one of the largest and wettest discoveries ever made, and, though this occurred over three centuries ago, Spain is still poor.

Balboa, in discovering the Pacific, did so according to the Spanish custom of discovery, viz., by wading into it with his naked sword in one hand and the banner of Castile, sometimes called Castile's hope (see Appendix), in the other. He and his followers waded out so as to discover all they could, and were surprised to discover what is now called the undertow.

BALBOA DRYING HIS CLOTHES.

The artist has shown the great discoverer most truthfully as he appeared after he had discovered and filed on the ocean. No one can look upon this picture for a moment and confuse Balboa, the discoverer of the Pacific, with Kope Elias, who first discovered in the mountains of North Carolina what is now known as moonshine whiskey.

De Narvaez in 1528 undertook to conquer Florida with three hundred hands. He also pulled considerable grass in his search for gold. Finally he got to the gulf and was wrecked. They were all related mostly to Narvaez, and for two weeks they lived on their relatives, but later struck shore—four of them—and lived more on a vegetable diet after that till they struck the Pacific Ocean, which now belonged to Spain.

De Soto also undertook the conquest of Florida after this, and took six hundred men with him for the purpose. They wandered through the Gulf States to the Mississippi, enduring much, and often forced to occupy the same room at night. De Soto in 1541 discovered the Mississippi River, thus adding to the moisture collection of Spain.

After trying to mortgage his discovery to Eastern capitalists, he died, and was buried in the quiet bosom of the Great Father of waters.

Thus once more the list of fatalities was added to and the hunger for gold was made to contribute a discovery.

Menendez later on founded in 1565 the colony of St. Augustine, the oldest town in the United States. There are other towns that look older, but it is on account of dissipation. New York looks older, but it is because she always sat up later of nights than St. Augustine did.

Cortez was one of the coarsest men who visited this country. He did not marry any wealthy American girls, for there were none, but he did everything else that was wrong, and his unpaid laundry-bills are still found all over the Spanish-speaking countries. He was especially lawless and cruel to the Peruvians: 'recognizing the Peruvian at once by his bark,' he would treat him with great indignity, instead of using other things which he had with him. Cortez had a way of capturing the most popular man in a city, and then he would call on the tax-payers to redeem him on the instalment plan. Most everybody hated Cortez, and when he held religious services the neighbors did not attend. The religious efforts made by Cortez were not successful. He killed a great many people, but converted but few.

The historian desires at this time to speak briefly of the methods of Cortez from a commercial stand-point.

Will the reader be good enough to cast his eye on the Cortez securities as shown in the picture drawn from memory by an artist yet a perfect gentleman?

BANK OF CORTEZ.

Notice the bonds Nos. 18 and 27. Do you notice the listening attitude of No. 18? He is listening to the accumulating interest. Note the aged and haggard look of No. 27. He has just begun to notice that he is maturing.

Cast your eye on the prone form of No. 31. He has just fallen due, and in doing so has hurt his crazy-bone (see Appendix).

Be good enough to study the gold-bearing bond behind the screen. See the look of anguish. Some one has cut off a coupon probably. Cortez was that kind of a man. He would clip the ear of an Inca and make him scream with pain, so that his friends would come in and redeem him. Once the bank examiner came to examine the Cortez bank. He imparted a pleasing flavor on the following day to the soup.

Spain owned at the close of the sixteenth century the West Indies, Yucatan, Mexico, and Florida, besides unlimited water facilities and the Peruvian preserves.

North Carolina was discovered by the French navigator Verrazani, thirty years later than Cabot did, but as Cabot did not record his claim at the court-house in Wilmington the Frenchman jumped the claim in 1524, and the property remained about the same till again discovered by George W. Vanderbilt in the latter part of the present century.

Montreal was discovered in 1535 by Cartier, also a Frenchman.

Ribaut discovered South Carolina, and left thirty men to hold it. They were at that time the only white men from-Mexico to the North Pole, and a keen business man could have bought the whole thing, Indians and all, for a good team and a jug of nepenthe. But why repine?

CONVERTING INDIANS.

The Jesuit missionaries about the middle of the seventeenth century pushed their way to the North Mississippi and sought to convert the Indians. The Jesuits deserve great credit for their patience, endurance, and industry, but they were shocked to find the Indian averse to work. They also advanced slowly in church work, and would often avoid early mass that they might catch a mess of trout or violate the game law by killing a Dakotah in May.

Father Marquette discovered the Upper Mississippi not far from a large piece of suburban property owned by the author, north of Minneapolis. The ground has not been disturbed since discovered by Father Marquette.

COULD NOT REACH THEM.

The English also discovered America from time to time, the Cabots finding Labrador while endeavoring to go to Asia via the North, and Frobisher discovered Baffin Bay in 1576 while on a like mission. The Spanish discovered the water mostly, and England the ice belonging to North America.

Sir Francis Drake also discovered the Pacific Ocean, and afterward sailed an English ship on its waters, discovering Oregon.

Sir Walter Raleigh, with the endorsement of his half-brother, Sir Humphrey Gilbert, regarding the idea of colonization of America, and being a great friend of Queen Elizabeth, got out a patent on Virginia.

He planted a colony and a patch of tobacco on Roanoke Island, but the colonists did not care for agriculture, preferring to hunt for gold and pearls. In this way they soon ran out of food, and were constantly harassed by Indians.

It was an odd sight to witness a colonist coming home after a long hard day hunting for pearls as he asked his wife if she would be good enough to pull an arrow out of some place which he could not reach himself.

Raleigh spent two hundred thousand dollars in his efforts to colonize Virginia, and then, disgusted, divided up his patent and sold county rights to it at a pound apiece. This was in 1589. Raleigh learned the use of smoking tobacco at this time.

RALEIGH'S ASTONISHMENT.

He was astonished when he tried it first, and threatened to change his boarding-place or take his meals out, but soon enjoyed it, and before he had been home a week Queen Elizabeth thought it to be an excellent thing for her house plants. It is now extensively used in the best narcotic circles.

RALEIGH'S ENJOYMENT.

Several other efforts were made by the English to establish colonies in this country, but the Indians thought that these English people bathed too much, and invited perspiration between baths.

One can see readily that the Englishman with his portable bath-tub has been a flag of defiance from the earliest discoveries till this day.

This chapter brings us to the time when settlements were made as follows:

The French at Port Royal, N.S.,	1605.
The English at Jamestown	1607.
The French at Quebec	1608.
The Dutch at New York	1613.
The English at Plymouth	1620.

The author's thanks are due to the following books of reference, which, added to his retentive memory, have made the foregoing statements accurate yet pleasing:

A Summer in England with H. W. Beecher. By J. B. Reed.

Russell's Digest of the Laws of Minnesota, with Price-List of Members.

Out-Door and Bug Life in America. By Chilblainy, Chief of the Umatilla.

Why I am an Indian. By S. Bull. With Notes by Ole Bull and Introduction by John Bull.

BONA FIDE PICTURE OF THE MAYFLOWER.

CHAPTER III.

THE THIRTEEN ORIGINAL COLONIES.

This chapter is given up almost wholly to facts. It deals largely with the beginning of the thirteen original colonies from which sprang the Republic, the operation of which now gives so many thousands of men in-door employment four years at a time, thus relieving the penitentiaries and throwing more kindergarten statesmen to the front.

SAMPLE PURITAN.

It was during this epoch that the Cavaliers landed in Virginia and the Puritans in Massachusetts; the latter lived on maple sugar and armed prayer, while the former saluted his cow, and, with bared head, milked her with his hat in one hand and his life in the other.

Immigration now began to increase along the coast. The Mayflower began to bring over vast quantities of antique furniture, mostly hall-clocks for future sales. Hanging them on spars and masts during rough weather easily accounts for the fact that none of them have ever been known to go.

The Puritans now began to barter with the Indians, swapping square black bottles of liquid hell for farms in Massachusetts and additions to log towns. Dried apples and schools began to make their appearance. The low retreating forehead of the codfish began to be seen at the stores, and virtue began to break out among the Indians after death.

Virginia, however, deserves mention here on the start. This colony was poorly prepared to tote wood and sleep out-of-doors, as the people were all gents by birth. They had no families, but came to Virginia to obtain fortunes and return to the city of New York in September. The climate was unhealthy, and before the first autumn, says Sir William Kronk, from whom I quote, 'ye greater numberr of them hade perished of a great Miserrie in the Side and for lacke of Food, for at thatte time the Crosse betweene the wilde hyena and the common hogge of the Holy Lande, and since called the Razor Backe Hogge, had not been made, and so many of the courtiers dyede.'

John Smith saved the colony. He was one of the best Smiths that ever came to this country, which is as large an encomium as a man cares to travel with. He would have saved the life of Pocahontas, an Indian girl who also belonged to the gentry of their tribe, but she saw at once that it would be a point for her to save him, so after a month's rehearsal with her father as villain, with Smith's part taken by a chunk of blue-gum wood, they succeeded in getting this little curtain-raiser to perfection.

Pocahontas was afterwards married, if the author's memory does not fail him, to John Rolfe. Pocahontas was not beautiful, but many good people sprang from her. She never touched them. Her husband sprang from her also just in time. The way she jumped from a clay-eating crowd into the bosom of the English aristocracy by this dramatic ruse was worthy of a greater recognition than merely to figure among the makers of smoking-tobacco with fancy wrappers, when she never had a fancy wrapper in her life.

THE REHEARSAL.

Smith was captured once by the Indians, and, instead of telling them that he was by birth a gent, he gave them a course of lectures on the use of the compass and how to learn where one is at. Thus one after another the Indians went away. I often wonder why the lecture is not used more as a means of escape from hostile people.

By writing a letter and getting a reply to it, he made another hit. He now became a great man among the Indians; and to kill a dog and fail to invite Smith to the symposium was considered as vulgar as it is now to rest the arctic overshoe on the corner of the dining-table while buckling or unbuckling it.

Afterward Smith fell into the hands of Powhatan, the Croker of his time, and narrowly saved his life, as we have seen, through the intervention of Pocahontas.

Smith was now required in England to preside at a dinner given by the Savage Club, and to tell a few stories of life in the Far West.

While he was gone the settlement became a prey to disease and famine. Some were killed by the Indians while returning from their club at evening; some became pirates.

The colony decreased from four hundred and ninety to sixty people, and at last it was moved and seconded that they do now adjourn. They started away from Jamestown without a tear, or hardly anything else, having experienced a very dull time there, funerals being the only relaxation whatever.

But moving down the bay they met Lord Delaware, the new Governor, with a lot of Christmas-presents and groceries. Jamestown was once more saved, though property still continued low. The company, by the terms of its new charter, became a self-governing institution, and London was only too tickled to get out of the responsibility. It is said that the only genuine humor up to that time heard in London was spent on the jays of Jamestown and the Virginia colony.

Where is that laughter now? Where are the gibes and *bon-mots* made at that sad time?

They are gone.

All over that little republic, so begun in sorrow and travail, there came in after-years the dimples and the smiles of the prosperous child who would one day rise in the lap of the mother-country, and, asserting its rights by means of Patrick O'Fallen Henry and others, place a large and disagreeable fire-cracker under the nose of royalty, that, busting the awful stillness, should jar the empires of earth, and blow the unblown noses of future kings and princes. (This is taken bodily from a speech made by me July 4, 1777, when I was young. — THE AUTHOR.)

Pocahontas was married in 1613. She was baptized the day before. Whoever thought of that was a bright and thoughtful thinker. She stood the wear and tear of civilization for three years, and then died, leaving an infant son, who has since grown up.

NEGROES STILL HAVE FAMILIES.

The colony now prospered. All freemen had the right to vote. Religious toleration was enjoyed first-rate, and, there being no negro slavery, Virginia bade fair to be *the* republic of the continent. But in 1619 the captain of a Dutch trading-vessel sold to the colonists twenty negroes. The negroes were mostly married people, and in some instances children were born to them. This peculiarity still shows itself among the negroes, and now all over the South one hardly crosses a county without seeing a negro or a person with negro blood in his or her veins.

After the death of Powhatan, the friend of the English, an organized attempt was made by the Indians to exterminate the white people and charge more for water frontage the next time any colonists came.

PREPARING THE FEAST.

March 22, 1622, was the day set, and many of the Indians were eating at the tables of those they had sworn to kill. It was a solemn moment. The surprise was to take place between the cold beans and the chili sauce.

But a converted Indian told quite a number, and as the cold beans were passed, the effect of some arsenic that had been eaten with the slim-neck clams began to be seen, and before the beans had gone half-way round the board the children of the forest were seen to excuse themselves, and thus avoid dying in the house.

Yet there were over three hundred and fifty white people massacred, and there followed another, reducing the colonists from four thousand to two thousand five hundred, then a massacre of five hundred, and so on, a sickening record of death and horror, even worse, before a great nation could get a foothold in this wild and savage land; even a toe-hold, as I may say, in the sands of time.

July 30, 1619, the first sprout of Freedom poked its head from the soil of Jamestown when Governor Yeardley stated that the colony 'should have a handle in governing itself.' He then called at Jamestown the first legislative body ever assembled in America; most of the members whereof boarded at the Planters' House during the session. (For sample of legislator see picture.) This body could pass laws, but they must be ratified by the company in England. The orders from London were not binding unless ratified by this Colonial Assembly.

This was a mutual arrangement reminding one of the fearful yet mutual apprehension spoken of by the poet when he says,—

'Jim Darling didn't know but his father was dead, And his father didn't know but Jim Darling was dead.'

The colony now began to prosper; men held their lands in severalty, and taxes were low. The railroad had not then brought in new styles in clothing and made people unhappy by creating jealousy.

Settlements joined each other along the James for one hundred and forty miles, and the colonists first demonstrated how easily they could get along without the New York papers.

Tobacco began to be a very valuable crop, and at one time even the streets were used for its cultivation. Tobacco now proceeded to become a curse to the civilized world.

JAMESTOWN LEGISLATOR.

In 1624, King James, fearing that the infant colony would go Democratic, appointed a rump governor.

The oppression of the English parliament now began to be felt. The colonists were obliged to ship their products to England and to use only English vessels. The Assembly, largely royalists, refused to go out when their terms of office expired, paid themselves at the rate of about thirty-six dollars per day as money is now, and, in fact, acted like members of the Legislature generally.

In 1676, one hundred years before the Colonies declared themselves free and independent, a rebellion, under the management of a bright young attorney named Bacon, visited Jamestown and burned the American metropolis, after which Governor Berkeley was driven out. Bacon died just as his rebellion was beginning to pay, and the people dispersed. Berkeley then took control, and killed so many rebels that Mrs. Berkeley had to do her own work, and Berkeley, who had no one left to help him but his friends, had to stack his own grain that fall and do the chores at the barn.

Jamestown is now no more. It was succeeded in 1885 by Jamestown, North Dakota, now called Jimtown, a prosperous place in the rich farming-lands of that State.

Jamestown the first, the scene of so many sorrows and little jealousies, so many midnight Indian attacks and bilious attacks by day, became a solemn ruin, and a few shattered tombstones, over which the jimson-weed and the wild vines clamber, show to the curious traveller the place where civilization first sought to establish itself on the James River, U.S.A.

The author wishes to refer with great gratitude to information contained in the foregoing chapter and obtained from the following works:

The Indian and other Animalcula. By N. K. Boswell, Laramie City, Wyoming.

How to Jolly the Red Man out of his Lands. By Ernest Smith.

The Female Red Man and her Pure Life. By Johnson Sides, Reno, Nevada (P.M. please forward if out on war-path).

The Crow Indian and His Caws. By Me.

Massacre Etiquette. By Wad. McSwalloper, 82 McDougall St., New York.

Where is my Indian to night? By a half-bred lady of Winnipeg.

CHAPTER IV.

THE PLYMOUTH COLONY.

In the fall of 1620 the Pilgrims landed at Plymouth during a disagreeable storm, and, noting the excellent opportunity for future misery, began to erect a number of rude cabins. This party consisted of one hundred and two people of a resolute character who wished to worship God in a more extemporaneous manner than had been the custom in the Church of England.

SABBATH-BREAKER ARRESTER.

They found that the Indians of Cape Cod were not ritualistic, and that they were willing to dispose of inside lots at Plymouth on reasonable terms, retaining, however, the right to use the lands for massacre purposes from time to time.

The Pilgrims were honest, and gave the Indians something for their land in almost every instance, but they put a price upon it which has made the Indian ever since a comparatively poor man.

Half of this devoted band died before spring, and yet the idea of returning to England did not occur to them. 'No,' they exclaimed, 'we will not go back to London until we can go first-class, if we have to stay here two hundred years.'

During the winter they discovered why the lands had been sold to them so low. The Indians of one tribe had died there of a pestilence the year before, and so when the Pilgrims began to talk trade they did not haggle over prices.

PURITAN SNORE ARRESTER.

In the early spring, however, they were surprised to hear the word 'Welcome' proceeding from the door-mat of Samoset, an Indian whose chief was named Massasoit. A treaty was then made for fifty years, Massasoit taking 'the same.'

Canonicus once sent to Governor Bradford a bundle of arrows tied up in a rattlesnake's skin. The Governor put them away in the pantry with his other curios, and sent Canonicus a few bright new bullets and a little dose of powder. That closed the correspondence. In those days there were no newspapers, and most of the fighting was done without a guarantee or side bets.

Money-matters; however, were rather panicky at the time, and the people were kept busy digging clams to sustain life in order to raise Indian corn enough to give them sufficient strength to pull clams enough the following winter to get them through till the next corn crop should give them strength to dig for clams again. Thus a trip to London and the Isle of Wight looked farther and farther away.

After four years they numbered only one hundred and eighty-four, counting immigration and all. The colony only needed, however, more people and Eastern capital.

METHODS OF PUNISHMENT.

It would be well to pause here and remember the annoyances connected with life as a forefather. Possibly the reader has considered the matter already. Imagine how nervous one may be waiting in the hall and watching with a keen glance for the approach of the physician who is to announce that one is a forefather. The amateur forefather of 1620 must have felt proud yet anxious about the clam-yield also, as each new mouth opened on the prospect.

Cold!

Speaking of clams, it is said by some of the forefathers that the Cape Cod menu did not go beyond codfish croquettes until the beginning of the seventeenth century, when pie was added by act of legislature.

Clams are not so restless if eaten without the brisket, which is said to lie hard on the stomach.[2]

Salem and Charlestown were started by Governor Endicott, and Boston was founded in 1630. To

Hunger!!

these various towns the Puritans flocked, and even now one may be seen in ghostly garments on Thanksgiving Eve flitting here and there turning off the gas in the parlor while the family are at tea, in order to cut down expenses.

Plymouth and Massachusetts Bay Colonies were united in 1692.

Roger Williams, a bright young divine, was the first to interfere with the belief that magistrates had the right to punish Sabbath-breakers, blasphemers, etc. He also was the first to utter the idea that a man's own conscience must be his own guide and not that of another.

Injuns!!!

Among the Puritans there were several who had enlarged consciences, and who desired to take in extra work for others who had no consciences and were busy in the fields. They were always ready to give sixteen ounces to the pound, and were honest, but they got very little rest on Sunday, because they had to watch the Sabbath-breaker all the time.

The method of punishment for some offences is given here.

Does the man look cheerful? No. No one looks cheerful. Even the little boys look sad. It is said that the Puritans knocked what fun there was out of the Indian. Did any one ever see an Indian smile since the landing of the Pilgrims?

Roger Williams was too liberal to be kindly received by the clergy, and so he was driven out of the settlement. Finding that the Indians were less rigid and kept open on Sundays, he took refuge among them (1636), and before spring had gained eighteen pounds and converted Canonicus, one of the hardest cases in New England and the first man to sit up till after ten o'clock at night. Canonicus gave Roger the tract of land on which Providence now stands.

Mrs. Anne Hutchinson gave the Pilgrims trouble also. Having claimed some special revelations and attempted to make a few remarks regarding them, she was banished.

Banishment, which meant a homeless life in a wild land, with no one but the Indians to associate with, in those days, was especially annoying to a good Christian woman, and yet it had its good points. It offered a little religious freedom, which could not be had among those who wanted it so much that they braved the billow and the wild beast, the savage, the drouth, the flood, and the potato-bug, to obtain it before anybody else got a chance at it. Freedom is a good thing.

Twenty years later the Quakers shocked every one by thinking a few religious thoughts on their own hooks. The colonists executed four of them, and before that tortured them at a great rate.

During dull times and on rainy days it was a question among the Puritans whether they would banish an old lady, bore holes with a red-hot iron through a Quaker's tongue, or pitch horse-shoes.

In 1643 the 'United Colonies of New England' was the name of a league formed by the people for protection against the Indians.

King Philip's war followed.

Massasoit was during his lifetime a friend to the poor whites of Plymouth, as Powhatan had been of those at Jamestown, but these two great chiefs were succeeded by a low set of Indians, who showed as little refinement as one could well imagine.

Some of the sufferings of the Pilgrims at the time are depicted on the preceding pages by the artist, also a few they escaped.

Looking over the lives of our forefathers who came from England, I am not surprised that, with all the English people who have recently come to this country, I have never seen a forefather.

CHAPTER V.

DRAWBACKS OF BEING A COLONIST.

It was at this period in the history of our country that the colonists found themselves not only banished from all civilization, but compelled to fight an armed foe whose trade was war and whose music was the dying wail of a tortured enemy. Unhampered by the exhausting efforts of industry, the Indian, trained by centuries of war upon adjoining tribes, felt himself foot-loose and free to shoot the unprotected forefather from behind the very stump fence his victim had worked so hard to erect.

King Philip, a demonetized sovereign, organized his red troops, and, carrying no haversacks, knapsacks, or artillery, fell upon the colonists and killed them, only to reappear at some remote point while the dead and wounded who fell at the first point were being buried or cared for by rude physicians.

What an era in the history of a country! Gentlewomen whose homes had been in the peaceful hamlets of England lived and died in the face of a cruel foe, yet prepared the cloth and clothing for their families, fed them, and taught them to look to God in all times of trouble, to be prayerful in their daily lives, yet vigilant and ready to deal death to the general enemy. They were the mothers whose sons and grandsons laid the huge foundations of a great nation and cemented them with their blood.

At this time there was a line of battle three hundred miles in length. On one side the white man went armed to the field or the prayer-meeting, shooting an Indian on sight as he would a panther; on the other, a foe whose wife did the chores and hoed the scattering crops while he made war and extermination his joy by night and his prayer and life-long purpose by day.

PRAYERFUL YET VIGILANT.

Finally, however, the victory came sluggishly to the brave and deserving. One thousand Indians were killed at one pop, and their

wigwams were burned. All their furniture and curios were burned in their wigwams, and some of their valuable dogs were holocausted. King Philip was shot by a follower as he was looking under the throne for something, and peace was for the time declared.

About 1684 the Colony of Massachusetts, which had dared to open up a trade with the West Indies, using its own vessels for that purpose, was hauled over the coals by the mother-country for violation of the Navigation Act, and an officer

AN OVATION IN THE WAY OF
EGGS AND CODFISH.

sent over to enforce the latter. The colonists defied him, and when he was speaking to them publicly in a tone of reprimand, he got an ovation in the way of eggs and codfish, both of which had been set aside for that purpose when the country was new, and therefore had an air of antiquity which cannot be successfully imitated.

As a result, the Colony was made a royal appendage, and Sir Edmund Andros, a political hack under James II., was made Governor of New England. He reigned under great difficulties for three years, and then suddenly found himself in jail. The jail was so arranged that he could not get out, and so the Puritans now quietly resumed their old form of government.

This continued also for three years, when Sir William Phipps became Governor under the crown, with one hundred and twenty pounds per annum and house-rent.

From this on to the Revolution, Massachusetts, Maine, and Nova Scotia became a royal province. Nova Scotia is that way yet, and has to go to Boston for her groceries.

The year 1692 is noted mostly for the Salem excitement regarding witchcraft. The children of Rev. Mr. Parris were attacked with some peculiar disease which would not yield to the soothing blisters and bleedings administered by the physicians of the old school, and so, not knowing exactly what to do about it, the doctors concluded that they were bewitched. Then it was, of course, the duty of the courts and selectmen to hunt up the witches. This was naturally difficult.

Fifty-five persons were tortured and twenty were hanged for being witches; which proves that the people of Salem were fully abreast of the Indians in intelligence, and that their gospel privileges had not given their charity and Christian love such a boom as they should have done.

OPENING OF THE WITCH-HUNTING SEASON.

One can hardly be found now, even in Salem, who believes in witchcraft; though the Cape Cod people, it is said, still spit on their bait. The belief in witchcraft in those days was not confined by any means to the colonists. Sir Matthew Hale of England, one of the most enlightened judges of the mother-country, condemned a number of people for the offence, and is now engaged in doing road-work on the streets of the New Jerusalem as a punishment for these acts done while on the woolsack.

Blackstone himself, one of the dullest authors ever read by the writer of these lines, yet a skilled jurist, with a marvellous memory regarding Justinian, said that, to deny witchcraft was to deny revelation.

'Be you a witch?' asked one of the judges of Massachusetts, according to the records now on file in the State-House at Boston.

'No, your honor,' was the reply.

'Officer,' said the court, taking a pinch of snuff, 'take her out on the tennis-grounds and pull out her toe-nails with a pair of hot pincers, and then see what she says.'

IRISHMAN WHO, WHEN RICH,
WAS PROUD AND HAUGHTY.

It was quite common to examine lady witches in the regular court and then adjourn to the tennis-court. A great many were ducked by order of the court and hanged up by the thumbs, in obedience to the customs of these people who came to America because they were persecuted.

Human nature is the same even to this day. The writer grew up with an Irishman who believed that when a man got wealthy enough to keep a carriage and coachman he ought to be assassinated and all his goods given to the poor. He now hires a coachman himself, having succeeded in New York city as a policeman; but the man who comes to assassinate him will find it almost impossible to obtain an audience with him.

IRISHMAN WHO, WHEN POOR,
WAS DOWN ON RICH PEOPLE.

If you wish to educate a man to be a successful oppressor, with a genius for introducing new horrors and novelties in pain, oppress him early in life and don't give him any reason for doing so. The idea that 'God is love' was not popular in those days. The early settlers were so stern even with their own children that if the Indian had not given the forefather something to attract his attention, the boy crop would have been very light.

Even now the philosopher is led to ask, regarding the boasted freedom of America, why some measures are not taken to put large fly-screens over it.

CHAPTER VI.

THE EPISODE OF THE CHARTER OAK.

The Colonies of Maine and New Hampshire were so closely associated with that of Massachusetts that their history up to 1820 was practically the same.

Shortly after the landing of the Pilgrims, say two years or thereabouts, Gorges and Mason obtained from England the grant of a large tract lying between the Merrimac and Kennebec Rivers. This patent was afterwards dissolved, Mason taking what is now New Hampshire, and Gorges taking Maine. He afterwards sold the State to Massachusetts for six thousand dollars. The growth of the State may be noticed since that time, for one county cost more than that last November.

In 1820 Maine was separated from Massachusetts. Maine is noted for being the easternmost State in the Union, and has been utilized by a number of eminent men as a birthplace. White-birch spools for thread, Christmas-trees, and tamarack and spruce-gum are found in great abundance. It is the home of an industrious and peace-loving people. Bar Harbor is a cool place to go to in summer-time and violate the liquor law of the State.

The Dutch were first to claim Connecticut. They built a trading-post at Hartford, where they swapped bone collar-buttons with the Indians for beaver-and otter-skins. Traders from Plymouth who went up the river were threatened by the Dutch, but they pressed on and established a post at Windsor.

In 1635, John Steele led a company 'out west' to Hartford, and Thomas Hooker, a clergyman, followed with his congregation, driving their stock before them. Hartford thus had quite a boom quite early in the seventeenth century. The Dutch were driven out of the Connecticut Valley, and began to look towards New York.

SEDUCTIONS OF BAR HARBOR.

Soon after this the Pequod War broke out. These Indians had hoped to form an alliance with the Narragansetts, but Roger Williams prevented this by seeing the Narragansett chief personally. Thus the Puritans had coals of fire heaped on their heads by their gentle pastor, until the odor of burning hair could be detected as far away as New Haven.

**PEQUOD INDIAN
ON THE WAR-PATH.**

The Pequods were thus compelled to fight alone, and Captain Mason by a *coup d'état* surrounded their camp before daylight and entered the palisades with the Indian picket, who cried out 'Owanux! Owanux!' Meaning' Englishmen Englishmen.' Mason and his men killed these Pequods and burned their lodges to the ground. There has never been a prosperous Pequod lodge since. Those who escaped to the forest were shot down like jack-rabbits as they fled, and there has been no Pequoding done since that time.

The New Haven Colony was founded in 1638 by wealthy church members from abroad. They took the Bible as their standard and statute. They had no other law. Only church members could vote, which was different from the arrangements in New York City in after-years.

The Connecticut Colony had a regular constitution, said to have been the first written constitution ever adopted by the people, framed for the people by the people. It was at once prosperous, and soon bought out the Saybrook Colony.

GOVERNOR ANDROS.

In 1662 a royal charter was obtained which united the two above colonies and guaranteed to the people the rights agreed upon by them. It amounted to a duly-authenticated independence. A quarter of a century afterwards Governor Andros, in his other clothes and a reigning coat of red and gold trimmings, marched into the Assembly and demanded this precious charter.

A long debate ensued, and, according to tradition, while the members of the Assembly stood around the table taking a farewell look at the charter, one of the largest members of the house fell on the governor's breast and wept so copiously on his shirt-frill that harsh words were used by his Excellency; a general quarrel ensued, the lights went out, and when they were relighted the charter was gone.

Captain Wadsworth had taken it and concealed it in a hollow tree, since called the Charter Oak. After Andros was ejected from the Boston office, the charter was brought out again, and business under it was resumed.

Important documents, however, should not be, as a general thing, secreted in trees. The author once tried this while young, and when engaged to, or hoping to become engaged to, a dear one whose pa was a singularly coarse man and who hated a young man who came as a lover at his daughter's feet with nothing but a good education and his great big manly heart. He wanted a son-in-law with a brewery; and so he bribed the boys of the neighborhood to break up a secret correspondence between the two young people and bring the mail to him. This was the cause of many a heart-ache, and finally the marriage of the sweet young lady to a brewer who was mortgaged so deeply that he wandered off somewhere and never returned. Years afterwards the brewery needed repairs, and one of the large vats was found to contain all of the missing man that would not assimilate with the beer, — viz., his watch. Quite a number of people at that time quit the use of beer, and the author gave his hand in marriage to a wealthy young lady who was attracted by his gallantry and fresh young beauty.

Roger Williams now settled at Providence Plantation, where he was joined by Mrs. Hutchinson, who also believed that the church and state should not be united, but that the state should protect the church and that neither should undertake to boss the other. It was also held that religious qualifications should not be required of political aspirants, also that no man should be required to whittle his soul into a shape to fit the religious auger-hole of another.

This was the beginning of Rhode Island. She desired at once to join the New England Colony, but was refused, as she had no charter. Plymouth claimed also to have jurisdiction over Rhode Island. This was very much like Plymouth.

NYE'S CHARTER OAK.

Having banished Roger Williams and Mrs. Hutchinson to be skinned by the Pequods and Narragansetts over at Narragansett Pier, they went on about their business, flogging Quakers, also ducking old women who had lumbago, and burning other women who would not answer affirmatively when asked, 'Be you a witch?'

Then when Roger began to make improvements and draw the attention of Eastern capital to Rhode Island and to organize a State or Colony with a charter, Plymouth said, 'Hold on, Roger: religiously we have cast you out, to live on wild strawberries, clams, and Indians, but from a mercantile and political point of view you will please notice that we have a string which you will notice is attached to your wages and discoveries.'

DUCKING OLD WOMEN.

Afterwards, however, Roger Williams obtained the necessary funds from admiring friends with which to go to England and obtain a charter which united the Colonies yet gave to all the first official right to liberty of conscience ever granted in Europe or America. Prior to that a man's conscience had a brass collar on it with the royal arms engraved thereon, and was kept picketed out in the king's grounds. The owner could go and look at it on Sundays, but he never had the use of it.

With the advent of freedom of political opinion, the individual use of the conscience has become popularized, and the time is coming when it will grow to a great size under our wise institutions and fostering skies. Instead of turning over our consciences to the safety deposit company of a great political party or religious organization and taking the key in our pocket, let us have individual charge of this useful little instrument and be able finally to answer for its growth or decay.

The author wishes to extend his thanks for the use of books of reference used in the collection of the foregoing facts; among them, 'How to Pay Expenses though Single,' by a Social Leper, 'How to

Keep Well,' by Methuselah, 'Humor of Early Days,' by Job, 'Dangers of the Deep,' by Noah, 'General Peacefulness and Repose of the Dead Indian,' by General Nelson A. Miles, 'Gulliver's Travels,' and 'Life and Public Services of the James Boys.'

NYE IN HIS FAMILY GALLERY.

CHAPTER VII.

THE DISCOVERY OF NEW YORK.

The author will now refer to the discovery of the Hudson River and the town of New York *via* Fort Lee and the 125th Street Ferry.

New York was afterwards sold for twenty-four dollars,—the whole island. When I think of this I go into my family gallery, which I also use as a swear room, and tell those ancestors of mine what I think of them. Where were they when New York was sold for twenty-four dollars? Were they having their portraits painted by Landseer, or their deposition taken by Jeffreys, or having their Little Lord Fauntleroy clothes made?

Do not encourage them to believe that they will escape me in future years. Some of them died unregenerate, and are now, I am told, in a country where they may possibly be damned; and I will attend to the others personally.

Twenty-four dollars for New York! Why, my Croton-water tax on one house and lot with fifty feet four and one-fourth inches front is fifty-nine dollars and no questions asked. Why, you can't get a voter for that now.

Henry—or Hendrik—Hudson was an English navigator, of whose birth and early history nothing is known definitely, hence his name is never mentioned in many of the best homes in New York.

In 1607 he made a voyage in search of the Northwest Passage. In one of his voyages he discovered Cape Cod, and later on the Hudson River.

This was one hundred and seventeen years after Columbus discovered America; which shows that the discovering business was not pushed as it should have been by those who had it in charge.

Hudson went up the river as far as Albany, but, finding no one there whom he knew, he hastened back as far as 209th Street West, and anchored.

He discovered Hudson Bay and Hudson Strait, and made other journeys by water, though aquatting was then in its infancy. Afterwards his sailors became mutinous, and set Hendrik and his son, with seven infirm sailors, afloat.

Ah! Whom have we here? (See next page.)

It is Hendrik Hudson, who discovered the Hudson River.

Here he has just landed at the foot of 209th Street, New York, where he offered the Indians liquor, but they refused.

How 209th Street has changed!

The artist has been fortunate in getting the expression of the Indians in the act of refusing. Mr. Hudson's great reputation lies in the fact that he discovered the river which bears his name; but the thinking mind will at once regard the discovery of an Indian who does not drink as far more wonderful.

74

DISCOVERY OF TEMPERANCE INDIANS.

Some historians say that this especial delegation was swept away afterward by a pestilence, whilst others commenting on the incident maintain that Hudson lied.

It is the only historical question regarding America not fully settled by this book.

Nothing more was heard of him till he turned up in a thinking part in 'Rip Van Winkle.'

Many claims regarding the discovery of various parts of the United States had been previously made. The Cabots had discovered Labrador, the Spaniards the southern part of the United States; the Norsemen had discovered Minneapolis, and Columbus had discovered San Salvador and gone home to meet a ninety-day note due in Palos for the use of the Pinta, which he had hired by the hour.

But we are speaking of the discovery of New York.

About this time a solitary horseman might have been seen at West 209th Street, clothed in a little brief authority, and looking out to the west as he petulantly spoke in the Tammany dialect, then in the language of the blank-verse Indian. He began, 'Another day of anxiety has passed, and yet we have not been discovered! The Great Spirit tells me in the thunder of the surf and the roaring cataract of the Harlem that within a week we will be discovered for the first time.'

As he stands there aboard of his horse, one sees that he is a chief in every respect and in life's great drama would naturally occupy the middle of the stage. It was at this moment that Hudson slipped down the river from Albany past Fort Lee, and, dropping a nickel in the slot at 125th Street, weighed his anchor at that place. As soon as he had landed and discovered the city, he was approached by the chief, who said, 'We gates. I am one of the committee to show you our little town. I suppose you have a power of attorney, of course, for discovering us?'

'Yes,' said Hudson. 'As Columbus used to say when he discovered San Salvador, 'I do it by the right vested in me by my sovereigns.' 'That oversizes my pile by a sovereign and a half,' says one of the natives; and so, if you have not heard it, there is a good thing for one of your dinner-speeches here.'

'Very good,' said the chief, as they jogged down-town on a swift Sixth Avenue elevated train towards the wigwams on 14th Street, and going at the rate of four miles an hour. 'We do not care especially who discovers us, so long as we hold control of the city organization. How about that, Hank?'

'That will be satisfactory,' said Mr. Hudson, taking a package of imported cheese and eating it, so that they could have the car to themselves.

'We will take the departments, such as Police, Street-Cleaning, etc., etc., etc., while you and Columbus get your pictures on the currency and have your graves mussed up on anniversaries. We get the two-moment horses and the country châteaux on the Bronx. Sabe?'

'That is, you do not care whose portrait is on the currency,' said Hudson, 'so you get the currency.'

Said the man, 'That is the sense of the meeting.'

Thus was New York discovered *via* Albany and Fort Lee, and five minutes after the two touched glasses, the brim of the schoppin and the Manhattan cocktail tinkled together, and New York was inaugurated.

Obtaining a gentle and philanthropical gentleman who knew too well the city by gas-light, they saw the town so thoroughly that nearly every building in the morning wore a bright red sign which read—

Beware of Paint.

Regarding the question as to who has the right to claim the priority of discovery of New York, I unite with one of the ablest historians now living in stating that I do not know.

Here and there throughout the work of all great historians who are frank and honest, chapter after chapter of information like this will burst forth upon the eye of the surprised and delighted reader.

CLUB LIFE IN EARLY NEW YORK.

Society at the time of the discovery of the blank-verse Indian of America was crude. Hudson's arrival, of course, among older citizens soon called out those who desired his acquaintance, but he noticed that club life was not what it has since become, especially Indian club life.

He found a nation whose regular job was war and whose religion was the ever-present prayer that they might eat the heart of their enemy plain.

The Indian High School and Young Ladies' Seminary captured by Columbus, as shown in the pictures of his arrival at home and his presentation to the royal pair one hundred and seventeen years before this, it is said, brought a royal flush to the face of King Ferdie, who had been well brought up.

This can be readily understood when we remember that the Indian wore at court a court plaster, a parlor-lamp-shade in stormy weather, made of lawn grass, or a surcingle of front teeth.

They were shown also in all these paintings as graceful and beautiful in figure; but in those days when the Pocahontas girls went barefooted till the age of eighty-nine years, chewed tobacco, kept Lent all winter and then ate a brace of middle-aged men for Easter, the figure must have been affected by this irregularity of meals.

THE INDIAN GIRL OF STORY. — THE INDIAN GIRL OF FACT.

Unless the Pocahontas of the present day has fallen off sadly in her carriage and beauty, to be saved from death by her, as Smith was, and feel that she therefore had a claim on him, must have given one nervous prostration, paresis, and insomnia.

The Indian and the white race never really united or amalgamated outside of Canada. The Indian has always held aloof from us, and even as late as Sitting Bull's time that noted cavalry officer said to the author that the white people who simply came over in the Mayflower could not marry into his family on that ground. He wanted to know why they *had to* come over in the Mayflower.

BILL NYE CONVERSING WITH SITTING BULL.

'We were here,' said the aged warrior, as he stole a bacon-rind which I used for lubricating my saw, and ate it thoughtfully, 'we were here and helped Adam 'round up' and brand his animals. We are an old family, and never did manual labor. We are just as poor and proud and indolent as those who are of noble blood. We know we are of noble blood because we have to take sarsaparilla all the time. We claim to come by direct descent from Job, of whom the inspired writer says, —

'Old Job he was a fine young lad,
Sing Glory hallelujah.
His heart was good, but his blood was bad,
Sing Glory hallelujah.'[3]

CHAPTER VIII.

THE DUTCH AT NEW AMSTERDAM.

Soon after the discovery of the Hudson, Dutch ships began to visit that region, to traffic in furs with the Indians. Some huts were erected by these traders on Manhattan Island in 1613, and a trading-post was established in 1615. Relics of these times are frequently turned up yet on Broadway while putting in new pipes, or taking out old pipes, or repairing other pipes, or laying plans for yet other pipes, or looking in the earth to see that the original pipes have not been taken away.

Afterwards the West India Company obtained a grant of New Netherland, and New Amsterdam was fairly started. In 1626, Minuit, the first governor, arrived, and, as we have stated, purchased the entire city of New York of the Indians for twenty-four dollars.

Then trouble sprang up between the Dutch and the Swedes on the Delaware over the possession of Manhattan, and when the two tribes got to conversing with each other over their rights, using the mother-tongue on both sides, it reminded one of the Chicago wheat market when business is good. The English on the Connecticut also saw that Manhattan was going to boom as soon as the Indians could be got farther west, and that property would be high there.

Peter Stuyvesant was the last Dutch governor of New York. He was a relative of mine. He disliked the English very much. They annoyed him with their democratic ideas and made his life a perfect hell to him. He would be sorry to see the way our folks have since begun to imitate the English. I can almost see him rising in his grave to note how the Stuyvesants in full cry pursue the affrighted anise-seed bag, or with their coaching outfits go tooling along 'cross country, stopping at the inns on the way and unlimbering their portable bath-tubs to check them with the 'clark.'

STUYVESANT'S VISION.

Pete, you did well to die early. You would not have been happy here now.

While Governor Stuyvesant was in hot water with the English, the Swedes, and the Indians, a fleet anchored in the harbor and demanded the surrender of the place in the name of the Duke of York, who wished to use it for a game preserve. After a hot fight with his council, some of whom were willing even then to submit to English rule and hoped that the fleet might have two or three suits of tweed which by mistake were a fit and therefore useless to the owners, and that they might succeed in swapping furs for these, the governor yielded, and in 1664 New York became a British possession, named as above.

The English governors, however, were not popular. They were mostly political hacks who were pests at home and banished to New York, where the noise of the streets soon drove them to drink. For nine years this sort of thing went on, until one day a

Dutch fleet anchored near the Staten Island brewery and in the evening took the town.

However, in the year following, peace was restored between England and Holland, and New Amsterdam became New York again, also subject to the Tammany rule.

Andros was governor for a time, but was a sort of pompous tomtit, with a short breath and a large aquiline opinion of himself. He was one of the arrogant old pie-plants whose growth was fostered by the beetle-bellied administration at home. He went back on board the City of Rome one day, and did not return.

New York had a gleam of hope for civil freedom under the rule of the Duke of York and the county Democracy, but when the duke became James II. he was just like other people who get a raise of salary, and refused to be privately entertained by the self-made ancestry of the American.

He was proud and arrogant to a degree. He forbade legislation, and stopped his paper. New York was

at this time annexed to the New England Colony, and began keeping

DUKE OF YORK.

the Sabbath so vigorously that the angels had great difficulty in getting at it.

Nicholson, who was the lieutenant tool of iniquity for Andros, fled with him when democracy got too hot for them. Captain Leisler, supported by Steve Brodie and everything south of the Harlem, but bitterly opposed by the aristocracy, who were distinguished by their ability to use new goods in making their children's clothes, whereas the democracy had to make vests for the boys from the cast-off trousers of their fathers, governed the province until Governor Sloughter arrived.

Sloughter was another imported Smearkase in official life, and arrested Leisler at the request of an aristocrat who drove a pair of bang-tail horses up and down Nassau Street on pleasant afternoons and was afterwards collector of the port. Having arrested Leisler for treason, the governor was a little timid about executing him, for he had never really killed a man in his life, and he hated the sight of blood; so Leisler's enemies got the governor to take dinner with them, and mixed his rum, so that when he got ready to speak, his remarks were somewhat heterogeneous, and before he went home he had signed a warrant for Leisler's immediate execution.

GOVERNOR SLOUGHTER'S PAINFUL AWAKENING.

When he awoke in the morning at his beautiful home on Whitehall Street, the sun was gayly glinting the choppy waves of Buttermilk Channel, and by his watch, which had run down, he saw that it was one o'clock, but whether it was one o'clock A.M. or P.M. he did not know, nor whether it was next Saturday or Tuesday before last. Oh, how he must have felt!

His room was dark, the gas having gone out to get better air. He attempted to rise, but a chill, a throb, a groan, and back he lay hastily on the bed just as it was on the point of escaping him. Suddenly a thought came to him. It was not a great thought, but it was such a thought as comes to those who have been thoughtless. He called for a blackamoor slave from abroad who did chores for him, and ordered a bottle of cooking brandy, then some club soda he had brought from London with him. Next he drank a celery-glass of it, and after that he felt better. He then drank another.

'Keep out of the way of this bed, Julius,' he said. 'It is coming around that way again. Step to one side, Julius, please, and let the bed walk around and stretch its legs. I never saw a bed spread itself so,' he continued, seeming to enjoy his own Lancashire humor. 'All night I seemed to feel a great pain creeping over me, Julius,' he said, hesitatingly, again filling his celery-glass, 'but I see now that it was a counterpane.'

Eighty years after that, Sloughter was a corpse.

We should learn from this not to be too hasty in selecting our birthplaces. Had he been born in America, he might have been alive yet.

NYE AS A BOY READING ABOUT KIDD.

From this on the struggles of the people up to the time of the Revolution were enough to mortify the reader almost to death. I will not go over them again. It was the history of all the other Colonies; poor, proud, with large masses of children clustering about, and Indians lurking in the out-buildings. The mother-country was negligent, and even cruel. Her political offscourings were sent to rule the people. The cranberry-crops soured on the vines, and times were very scarce.

It was during this period that Captain William Kidd, a New York ship-master and anti-snapper from Mulberry Street, was sent out to overtake and punish a few of the innumerable pirates who then infested the high seas.

Studying first the character, life, and public services of the immoral pirate, and being perfectly foot-loose, his wife having eloped with her family physician, he determined to take a little whirl at the business himself, hoping thereby to escape the noise and heat of New York and obtain a livelihood while life lasted which would maintain him the remainder of his days unless death overtook him.

Dropping off at Boston one day to secure a supply of tobacco, he was captured while watching the vast number of street-cars on Washington Street. He was taken to England, where he was tried and ultimately hanged. His sudden and sickening death did much to discourage an American youth of great brilliancy who had up to 1868 intended to be a pirate, but who, stumbling across the 'Life and Times of Captain Kidd, and his Awful Death,' changed his whole course and became one of the ablest historians of the age in which he lived.

This should teach us to read the papers instead of loaning them to people who do not subscribe.

CAPTAIN KIDD ARRESTED.

Since the above was written, the account of the death of Governor Andros is flashed across the wires to us. *Verbum sap.* Also *In hoc signo vinces.*

The author wishes to express by this means his grateful acknowledgments to his friends and the public generally for the great turn-out and general sympathy bestowed upon his relative, the late Peter B. Stuyvesant, on the sad occasion of his funeral, which was said to be one of the best attended and most successful funerals before the war. Should any of his friends be caught in the same fix, the author will not only cheerfully turn out himself, but send all hands from his place that can be spared, also a six-seated wagon and a side-bar buggy.

CHAPTER IX.

SETTLEMENT OF THE MIDDLE STATES.

BERKELEY IN NEW JERSEY.

The present State of New Jersey was a part of New Netherland, and the Dutch had a trading-post at Bergen as early as 1618. After New Netherland passed into the hands of the Dutch, the Duke of York gave the land lying between the Hudson and the Delaware to Lord Berkeley and Sir George Carteret for Christmas.

The first permanent English settlement made in the State was at Elizabethtown, named so in honor of Sir George's first wife.

Berkeley sold his part to some English Quakers. This part was called West Jersey. He claimed that it was too far from town. It was very hard for a lord to clear up land, and Berkeley missed his evenings at the Savage Club, and his nose yearned for a good whiff of real old Rotten Row fog.

So many disputes arose regarding the title to Jersey that the whole thing finally reverted to the crown in 1702. When there was any trouble over titles in those days it was always settled by letting it revert to the crown. It has been some years now, however, since that has happened in this country.

Thirty-six years later New Jersey was set apart as a separate royal province, and became a railroad terminus and bathing-place.

Delaware was settled by the Swedes at Wilmington first, and called New Sweden. I am surprised that the Norsemen, who it is claimed made the first and least expensive summer at Newport, R. I., should not have clung to it.

They could have made a good investment, and in a few years would have been strong enough to wipe out the Brooklyn police.

CHEAPEST NEWPORT SEASON.

The Swedes, too, had a good foothold in New York, Jersey, and Delaware, also a start in Pennsylvania. But the two nations seemed to yearn for home, and as soon as boats began to run regularly to Stockholm and Christiania, they returned. In later years they discovered Minneapolis and Stillwater.

William Penn now loomed up on the horizon. He was an English Quaker who had been expelled from Oxford and jugged in Cork also for his religious belief. He was the son of Admiral Sir William Penn, and had a good record. He believed that elocutionary prayer was unnecessary, and that the acoustics of heaven were such that the vilest sinner with no voice-culture could be heard in the remotest portion of the gallery.

The only thing that has been said against Penn with any sort of semblance of truth was that he had some influence with James II. The Duke of York also stood in with Penn, and used to go about in England bailing William out whenever he was jailed on account of his religious belief.

Penn was quite a writer (see Appendix). He was the author of 'No Cross, No Crown,' 'Innocency with her Open Face,' and 'The Great Cause of Liberty of Conscience.'

From his father he had inherited a claim against the government for sixteen thousand pounds, probably arrears of pension. He finally received the State of Pennsylvania as payment of the claim. The western boundary took in the Cliff House and Seal Rocks of San Francisco.

Penn came to America in 1682 and bought his land over again from the Indians. It is not strange that he got the best terms he could out of the Indians, but still it is claimed that they were satisfied, therefore he did not cheat them.

The Indian, as will be noticed by reading these pages thoughtfully, was never a Napoleon of finance. He is that way down to the present day. If you watch him carefully and notice his ways, you can dicker with him to better advantage than you can with Russell Sage.

Take the Indian just before breakfast after two or three nights of debauchery, and offer him a jug of absinthe with a horned toad in it for his pony and saddle, and you will get them. Even in his more sober and thoughtful moments you can swap a suit of red medicated flannels with him for a farm.

Penn gathered about him many different kinds of people, with various sorts and shades of belief. Some were Free-Will and some were Hard-Shell, some were High-Church and reminded one of a Masonic Lodge working at 32°, while others were Low-Church and omitted crossing themselves frequently while putting down a new carpet in the chancel.

A FEW OF PENN'S PEOPLE.

But he was too well known at court, and suspected of knowledge of and participation in some of the questionable acts of King James, so that after the latter's dethronement, and an intimation that Penn had communicated with the exiled monarch, Penn was deprived of his title to Pennsylvania, for which he had twice paid.

Penn was a constant sufferer at the hands of his associates, who sought to injure him in every way. He rounded out a life of suffering by marrying the second time in 1695.

In 1708 he was on the verge of bankruptcy, owing to the villany and mismanagement of his agent, and was thrown into Fleet Street Prison, a jail in which he had never before been confined. His health gave way afterwards, and this remarkable man died July 30, 1718.

Philadelphia was founded in 1683 and work begun on a beautiful building known as the City Hall. Work has steadily progressed on this building from time to time since then, and at this writing it is so near completion as to give promise of being one of the most perfect architectural jobs ever done by the hand of man.

In two years Philadelphia had sprung from a wilderness, where the rank thistle nodded in the wind, to a town of over two thousand people, exclusive of Indians not taxed. In three years it had gained more than New York had in fifty years. This was due to the fact that the people who came to Philadelphia had nothing to fear but the Indians, while settlers in New York had not only the Indians to defend themselves against, but the police also.

Penn and his followers established the great law that no one who believed in Almighty God should be molested in his religious belief. Even the Indians liked Penn, and when the nights were cold they would come and crawl into his bed and sleep with him all night and not kill him at all. The Great Chief of the Tribes, even, did not feel above this, and the two used frequently to lie and talk for hours, Penn doing the talking and the chief doing the lying.

It is said that, with all the Indian massacres and long wars between the red men and the white, no drop of Quaker blood was ever shed. I quote this from an historian who is much older than I, and with whom I do not wish to have any controversy.

After Penn's death his heirs ran the Colony up to 1779, when they disposed of it for five hundred thousand dollars or thereabouts, and the State became the proprietor.

PENN AND THE BIG CHIEF.

The seventeenth century must have been a very disagreeable period for people who professed religion, for America from Newfoundland to Florida was dotted with little settlements almost entirely made up of people who had escaped from England to secure religious freedom at the risk of their lives.

In 1634 the first settlement was made by young Lord Baltimore, whose people, the Catholics, were fleeing from England to obtain freedom to worship God as they believed to be right. Thus the Catholics were added to the list of religious refugees,—viz., the Huguenots, the Puritans, the Walloons, the Quakers, the Presbyterians, the Whigs, and the Menthol Healers.

Terra Mariæ, or Maryland, was granted to Lord Baltimore, as the successor of his father, who had begun before his death the movement for settling his people in America. The charter gave to all freemen a voice in making the laws. Among the first laws passed was one giving to every human being upon payment of poll-tax the right to worship freely according to the dictates of his own conscience. America thus became the refuge for those who had any peculiarity of religious belief, until to-day no doubt more varieties of religion may be found here than almost anywhere else in the world.

In 1635 the Virginia Colony and Lord Baltimore had some words over the boundaries between the Jamestown and Maryland Colonies.

Clayborne was the Jamestown man who made the most trouble. He had started a couple of town sites on the Maryland tract, plotted them, and sold lots to Yorkshire tenderfeet, and so when Lord Baltimore claimed the lands Clayborne attacked him, and there was a running skirmish for several years, till at last the Rebellion collapsed in 1645 and Clayborne fled.

The Protestants now held the best hand, and outvoted the Catholics, so up to 1691 there was a never-dying fight between the two, which must have been entertaining to the unregenerate outsider who was taxed to pay for a double set of legislators. This fight between the Catholics and Protestants shows that intolerance is not confined to a monarchy.

In 1715 the fourth Lord Baltimore recovered the government by the aid of the police, and religious toleration was restored. Maryland remained under this system of government until the Revolution, which will be referred to later on in the most thrilling set of original pictures and word-paintings that the reader has ever met with.

QUESTIONS FOR EXAMINATION.

Q. Who was William Penn?

A. He founded Pennsylvania.

Q. Was he a great fighter?

A. No. He was a peaceable man, and did not believe in killing men or fighting.

Q. Would he have fought for a purse of forty thousand dollars?

A. No. He could do better buying coal lands of the Indians.

Q. What is religious freedom?

A. It is the art of giving intolerance a little more room.

Q. Who was Lord Baltimore?

A. See foregoing chapter.

Q. What do you understand by rebellion?

A. It is an unsuccessful attempt by armed subjects to overcome the parent government.

Q. Is it right or wrong?

A. I do not know, but will go and inquire.

CHAPTER X.

THE EARLY ARISTOCRACY.

Lord Clarendon and several other noblemen in 1663 obtained from Charles II. a grant of lands lying south of Virginia which they called Carolina in honor of the king, whose name was not really Carolina. Possibly that was his middle name, however, or his name in Latin.

The Albemarle Colony was first on the ground. Then there was a Carteret Colony in 1670. They 'removed the ancient groves covered with yellow jessamine' on the Ashley, and began to build on the present site of Charleston.

The historian remarks that the growth of this Colony was rapid from the first. The Dutch, dissatisfied with the way matters were conducted in New York, and worn out when shopping by the ennui and impudence of the salesladies, came to Charleston in large numbers, and the Huguenots in Charleston found a hearty Southern welcome, and did their trading there altogether.

We now pass on to speak of the Grand Model which was set up as a five-cent aristocracy by Lord Shaftesbury and the great philosopher John Locke. The canebrakes and swamps of the wild and snake-infested jungles of the wilderness were to be divided into vast estates, over which were proprietors with hereditary titles and outing flannels.

This scheme recognized no rights of self-government whatever, and denied the very freedom which the people came there in search of. So there were murmurings among those people who had not brought their finger-bowls and equerries with them.

In short, aristocracy did not do well on this soil. Baronial castles, with hot and cold water in them, were often neglected, because the colonists would not forsake their own lands to the thistle and blue-nosed brier in order to come and cook victuals for the baronial castles or sweep out the baronial halls and wax the baronial floors for a journeyman juke who ate custard pie with a knife and drank tea from his saucer through a King Charles moustache.

ARISTOCRACY SNUBBED.

Thus the aristocracy was forced to close its doors, and the arms of Lord Shaftesbury were so humiliated that he could no longer put up his dukes (see Appendix)

There had also been a great deal of friction between the Albemarle or Carteret and the Charleston set, the former being from Virginia, while the latter was, as we have seen, a little given to kindergarten aristocracy and ofttimes tripped up on their parade swords while at the plough. Of course outside of this were the plebeian people, or copperas-culottes, who did the work; but Lord Shaftesbury for some time, as we have seen, lived in a baronial shed and had his arms worked on the left breast of his nighty.

So these two Colonies finally became separate States in the Union, though there is yet something of the same feeling between the people. Wealthy people come to the mountains of North Carolina from South Carolina for the cool summer breezes of the Old

North State, and have to pay two dollars per breeze even up to the past summer.

TWO DOLLARS PER BREEZE.

Thus there was constant irritation and disgust up to 1729 at least, regarding taxes, rents, and rights, until, as the historian says, 'the discouraged Proprietors ceded their rights to the crown.'

It will be noticed that the crown was well ceded by this time, and the poet's remark seems at this time far grander and more apropos than any language of the writer could be: so it is given here,—viz., 'Uneasy lies the head that wears a seedy crown.' (see Appendix)

The year of Washington's birth, viz., 1732, witnessed the birth of the baby colony of Georgia. James Oglethorpe, a kind-hearted man, with a wig that fooled more than one poor child of the forest, conceived the idea of founding a refuge for Englishmen who could not pay up. The laws were very arbitrary then, and harsh to a degree. Many were imprisoned then in England for debt, but those who visit London now will notice that they are at liberty.

OGLETHORPE'S WIG.

Oglethorpe was an officer and a gentleman, and this scheme showed his generous nature and philanthropic disposition. George II. granted him in trust for the poor a tract of land called, in honor of the king, Georgie, which has recently been changed to Georgia. The enterprise prospered remarkably, and generous and charitable people aided it in every possible way. People who had not been able for years to pay their debts came to Georgia and bought large tracts of land or began merchandising with the Indians. Thousands of acres of rich cotton-lands were exchanged by the Indians for orders on the store, they giving warranty deeds to same, reserving only the rights of piscary and massacre.

Oglethorpe got along with the Indians first-rate, and won their friendship. One great chief, having received a present from Oglethorpe consisting of a manicure set, on the following Christmas gave Oglethorpe a beautiful buffalo robe, on the inside of which were painted an eagle and a portable bath-tub, signifying, as the chief stated, that the buffalo was the emblem of strength, the eagle of swiftness, and the bath-tub the advertisement of cleanliness. 'Thus,' said the chief, 'the English are strong as the buffalo, swift as the eagle, and love to convey the idea that they are just about to take a bath when you came and interrupted them.'

NOT PAID THEIR DEBTS FOR YEARS.

The Moravians also came to Georgia, and the Scotch Highlanders. On the arrival of the latter, the Georgia mosquitoes held a mass meeting, at which speeches were made, and songs sung, and resolutions adopted making the Highland uniform the approved costume for the entire coast during summer.

THE MOSQUITOES LIKED THE COSTUME.

George Whitefield the eloquent, who often addressed audiences (even in those days, when advertising was still in its infancy and the advance agent was unheard of) of from five thousand to forty thousand people, founded an orphan asylum. One audience consisted of sixty thousand people. The money from this work all went to help and sustain the orphan asylum. While reading of him we are reminded of our own Dr. Talmage, who is said to be the wealthiest apostle on the road.

The trustees of Georgia limited the size of a man's farm, did not allow women to inherit land, and forbade the importation of rum or of slaves. Several of these rules were afterwards altered, so that as late as 1893 at least a gentleman from Washington, D.C., well known for his truth and honesty, saw rum inside the State twice, though Bourbon whiskey was preferred. Slaves also were found inside the State, and the negro is seen there even now; but the popularity of a negro baby is nothing now to what it was at the time when this class of goods went up to the top notch.

Need I add that after a while the people became dissatisfied with these rules and finally the whole matter was ceded to the crown? From this time on Georgia remained a royal province up to the Revolution. Since that very little has been said about ceding it to the crown.

North Carolina also remained an English colony up to the same period, and, though one of the original thirteen Colonies, is still far more sparsely settled than some of the Western States.

Virginia Dare was the first white child born in America. She selected Roanoke, now in North Carolina, in August, 1587, as her birthplace. She was a grand-daughter of the Governor, John White. Her fate, like that of the rest of the colony, is unknown to this day.

The author begs leave to express his thanks here for the valuable aid furnished him by the following works,—viz.: 'The Horse and his Diseases,' by Mr. Astor; 'Life and Times of John Oglethorpe,' by Elias G. Merritt; 'How to Make the Garden Pay,' by Peter Henderson; 'Over the Purple Hills,' by Mrs. Churchill, of Denver, Colorado, and 'He Played on the Harp of a Thousand Strings, and the Spirits of Just Men Made Perfect,' by S. P. Avery.

CHAPTER XI.

INTERCOLONIAL AND INDIAN WARS.

Intercolonial and Indian wars furnished excitement now from 1689 into the early part of the eighteenth century. War broke out in Europe between the French and English, and the Colonies had to take sides, as did also the Indians.

Canadians and Indians would come down into York State or New England, burn a town, tomahawk quite a number of people, then go back on snow-shoes, having entered the town on rubbers, like a decayed show with no printing.

There was an attack on Haverhill in March, 1697, and a Mr. Dustin was at work in the field. He ran to his house and got his seven children ahead of him, while with his gun he protected their rear till he got them away safely. Mrs. Dustin, however, who ran back into the house to remove a pie from the oven as she feared it was burning, was captured, and, with a boy of the neighborhood, taken to an island in the Merrimac, where the Indians camped. At night she woke the boy, told him how to hit an Indian with a tomahawk so that 'the subsequent proceedings would interest him no more,' and that evening the two stole forth while the ten Indians slept, knocked in their thinks, scalped them to prove their story, and passed on to safety. Mrs. Dustin kept those scalps for many years, showing them to her friends to amuse them.

King William's War lasted eight years. Queen Anne's War lasted from 1702 to 1713. The brunt of this war fell on New England. Our forefathers had to live in block-houses, with barbed-wire fences around them, and carry their guns with them all the time. From planting the Indian with a shotgun, they soon got to planting their corn with the same agricultural instrument in the stony soil.

The French and Spanish tried to take Charleston in 1706, but were repulsed with great loss, consisting principally of time which they might have employed in raising frogs' legs and tantalizing a bull at so much per tant.

This war lasted eleven years, including stops, and was ended by the treaty of Utrecht (pronounced you-trecked).

After this, what was called the Spanish War continued between England and Spain for some time. An attempt to capture Georgia was made, and a garrison established itself there, with good prospects of taking in the State under Spanish rule, but our able friend Oglethorpe, the Henry W. Grady of his time, managed to accidentally mislay a letter which fell into the enemy's hands, the contents of which showed that enormous reinforcements were expected at any moment. This was swallowed comfortably by the commander, who blew up his impregnable works, changed the address of his *Atlanta Constitution*, and sailed for home.

Oglethorpe wore a wig, but was otherwise one of our greatest minds. It is said that anybody at a distance of two miles on a clear day could readily distinguish that it was a wig, and yet he died believing that no one had ever probed his great mystery and that his wig would rise with him at the playing of the last trump.

King George's War, which extended over four years, succeeded, but did not amount to anything except the capture of Cape Breton by English and Colonial troops. Cape Breton was called the Gibraltar of America; but a Yankee farmer who has raised flax on an upright farm for twenty years does not mind scaling a couple of Gibraltars before breakfast; so, without any West Point knowledge regarding they got

BELIEVING HIS
WIG
WOULD RISE
WITH HIM.

to the engineering, they walked up the hill, and those who were alive when and no dumb animal show, but simply revealed the fact that brave men fighting for their eight-dollar homes and a mass of children are disagreeable people to meet on the battle-field.

The French and Indian War lasted nine years,—viz., from 1754 to 1763. From Quebec to New Orleans the French owned the land, and mixed up a good deal socially with the Indians, so that the slender settlement along the coast had arrayed against it this vast line of northern and western forts, and the Indians, who were mostly friendly with the French, united with them in several instances and showed them some new styles of barbarism which up to that time they had never known about.

The half-breed is always half French and half Indian.

The English owned all lands lying on one side of the Ohio, the French on the other, which led a great chief to make a P. P. C. call on Governor Dinwiddie, and during the conversation to inquire with some *naïveté* where the Indian came in. No answer was ever received.

We pause here to ask the question, Why did the pale-face usurp the lands of the Indians without remuneration? It was because the Indian was not orthodox. He may have been lazy from a Puritanical stand-point, and he may also have hunted on the twenty-seventh Sunday after Easter; but still was it not right that he should have received a dollar or two per county for the United States? No one would have felt it, and possibly it might have saved the lives of innocent people.

Verbum sap., however, comes in here with peculiar appropriateness, and the massive-browed historian passes on.

The French had three forts along in the Middle States, as they are now called, and Western Pennsylvania; and George Washington, of whom more will be said in the twelfth chapter, was sent to ask the French to remove these forts. He started at once.

PLEASURE OF BEING ARRESTED IN PARIS.

The commanders were some of them arrogant, but the general, St. Pierre, treated him with great respect, refusing, however, to yield the ground discovered by La Salle and Marquette. The author had the pleasure of being arrested in Paris in 1889, and he feels of a truth, as he often does, that there can be no more polite people in the world than the French. Arrested under all circumstances and in many lands, the author can place his hand on his heart and say that he would go hundreds of miles to be arrested by a John Darm.

Washington returned four hundred miles through every kind of danger, including a lunch at Altoona, where he stopped twenty minutes.

The following spring Washington was sent under General Fry to drive out the French, who had started farming at Pittsburg. Fry died, and Washington took command. He liked it very much. After that Washington took command whenever he could, and soon rose to be a great man.

.The first expedition against Fort Duquesne (pronounced du-kane) was commanded by General Braddock, whose portrait we are able to give, showing him at the time he did not take Washington's advice in the Duquesne matter. Later we show him as he appeared after he had abandoned his original plans and immediately after not taking Washington's advice.

'The Indians,' said Braddock, 'may frighten Colonial troops, but they can make no impression on the king's regulars. We are alike impervious to fun or fear.'

GENERAL BRADDOCK SCORNING
WASHINGTON'S ADVICE

Braddock thought of fighting the Indians by manœuvring in large bodies, but the first body to be manœuvred was that of General Braddock, who perished in about a minute.

We give the reader, above, an idea of Braddock's soldierly bearing after he had been manœuvring a few times.

It was then that Washington took command, as was his custom, and began to fight the Indians and French as one would hunt varmints in Virginia.

Braddock's men fired by platoons into the trees and tore a few holes in the State line, but when most of the Colonial troops were dead the regulars presented their tournures to the foe and fled as far as Philadelphia, where they each took a bath and had some laundry-work done.

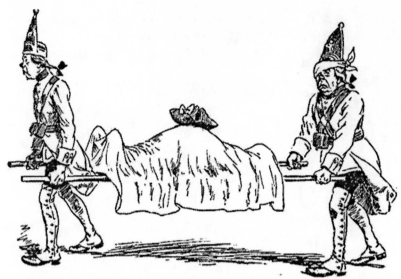

GENERAL BRADDOCK AFTER SCORNING WASHINGTON'S
ADVICE.

General Forbes took command of the second expedition. He spent
most of his time building roads.

Time passed on, and Forbes built viaducts, conduits, culverts, and
rustic bridges, till it was November, and they were yet fifty miles
from the fort. He then decided to abandon the expedition, on
account of the cold, and also fearing that he had not made all of his
bridges wide enough so that he could take the captured fort home
with him.

Washington, however, though only an aidy kong of General Forbes,
decided to take command. His mother had said to him over and
over, 'George, in an emergency always take command.' He done so,
as General Rusk would say. As he approached, the French set fire to
the fort, and retreated, together with the Indians and Molly
Maguires.

Pittsburg now stands on this historic ground, and is one of the most
delightful cities of America.

Many other changes were going on at this time. The English got possession of Acadia and the French forts at the head of the Bay of Fundy.

In 1757 General Loudon collected an army for an attack on Louisburg. He drilled his troops all summer, and then gave up the attack because he learned that the French had one more skiff than he had.

The Loudons of America at the time of this writing are more quiet and sensible regarding their ancestry than any of the doodle-bug aristocracy of our promoted peasantry and the crested Yahoos of our cowboy republic.

The Loudons—or Lowdowns—of America had a very large family. Some of them changed their names and moved.

The next year after the *fox pass* of General Loudon, Amherst and Wolfe took possession of the entire island.

About the time of Braddock's justly celebrated expedition another started out for Crown Point. The French, under Dieskau (pronounced dees-kow), met the army composed of Colonial troops in plain clothes, together with the regular troops led by officers with drawn swords and overdrawn salaries. The regular general, seeing that the battle was lost, excused himself and retired to his tent, owing to an ingrowing nail which had annoyed him all day. Lyman, the Colonial officer now took command, and wrung victory from the reluctant jaws of defeat. For this Johnson, the English general, received twenty-five thousand dollars and a baronetcy, while Lyman received a plated butter-dish and a bass-wood what-not. But Lyman was a married man, and had learned to take things as they came.

Four months prior to the capture of Duquesne, one thousand boats loaded with soldiers, each with a neat little lunch-basket and a little flag to wave when they hurrahed for the good kind man at the head of the picnic,—viz., General Abercrombie,—sailed down Lake George to get a whiff of fresh air and take Ticonderoga.

When they arrived, General Abercrombie took out a small book regarding tactics which he had bought on the boat, and, after refreshing his memory, ordered an assault. He then went back to see how his rear was, and, finding it all right, he went back still farther, to see if no one had been left behind.

ABERCROMBIE WENT BACK TO THE REAR.

Abercrombie never forgot or overlooked any one. He wanted all of his pleasure-party to be where they could see the fight.

In that way he missed it himself. I would hate to miss a fight that way.

The Abercrombies of America mostly trace their ancestry back by a cut-off avoiding the general's line.

Niagara had an expedition sent against it at the time of Braddock's trip. The commander was General Shirley, but he ran out of money while at the Falls and decided to return. This post did not finally surrender till 1759.

This gave the then West to the English. They had tried for one hundred and forty years to civilize it, but, alas, with only moderate success. Prosperous and happy even while sniping in their fox-hunting or canvas-back-duck clothes, these people feel somewhat soothed for their lack of culture because they are well-to-do.

In 1759 General Wolfe anchored off Quebec with his fleet and sent a boy up town to ask if there were any letters for him at the post-office, also asking at what time it would be convenient to evacuate the place. The reply came back from General Montcalm, an able French general, that there was no mail for the general, but if Wolfe was dissatisfied with the report he might run up personally and look over the W's.

Wolfe did so, taking his troops up by an unknown cow-path on the off side of the mountain during the night, and at daylight stood in battle-array on the Plains of Abraham. An attack was made by Montcalm as soon as he got over his wonder and surprise. At the third fire Wolfe was fatally wounded, and as he was carried back to the rear he heard some one exclaim, —

'They run! They run!'

'Who run?' inquired Wolfe.

'The French! The French!' came the reply.

'Now God be praised,' said Wolfe, 'I die happy.'

Montcalm had a similar experience. He was fatally wounded. 'They run! They run!' he heard some one say.

'Who run?' exclaimed Montcalm, wetting his lips with a lemonade-glass of cognac.

'We do,' replied the man.

'Then so much the better,' said Montcalm, as his eye lighted up, 'for I shall not live to see Quebec surrendered.'

This shows what can be done without a rehearsal; also how the historian has to control himself in order to avoid lying.

The death of these two brave men is a beautiful and dramatic incident in the history of our country, and should be remembered by every school-boy, because neither lived to write articles criticising the other.

Five days later the city capitulated. An attempt was made to recapture it, but it was not successful. Canada fell into the hands of the English, and from the open Polar Sea to the Mississippi the English flag floated.

What an empire!

What a game-preserve!

Florida was now ceded to the already cedy crown of England by Spain, and brandy-and-soda for the wealthy and bitter beer became the drink of the poor.

REMAINED BY IT TILL DEATH.

Pontiac's War was brought on by the Indians, who preferred the French occupation to that of the English. Pontiac organized a large number of tribes on the spoils plan, and captured eight forts. He killed a great many people, burned their dwellings, and drove out many more, but at last his tribes made trouble, as there were not spoils enough to go around, and his army was conquered. He was killed in 1769 by an Indian who received for his trouble a barrel of liquor, with which he began to make merry. He remained by the liquor till death came to his relief.

The heroism of an Indian who meets his enemy single-handed in that way, and, though greatly outnumbered, dies with his face to the foe, is deserving of more than a passing notice.

The French and Indian War cost the Colonists sixteen million dollars, of which the English repaid only five million. The Americans lost thirty thousand men, none of whom were replaced. They suffered every kind of horror and barbarity, written and unwritten, and for years their taxes were two-thirds of their income; and yet they did not murmur.

These were the fathers and mothers of whom we justly brag. These were the people whose children we are. What are inherited titles and ancient names many times since dishonored, compared with the heritage of uncomplaining suffering and heroism which we boast of to-day because those modest martyrs were working people, proud that by the sweat of their brows they wrung from a niggardly soil the food they ate, proud also that they could leave the plough to govern or to legislate, able also to survey a county or rule a nation.

CHAPTER XII.

PERSONALITY OF WASHINGTON.

It would seem that a few personal remarks about George Washington at this point might not be out of place. Later on his part in this history will more fully appear.

The author points with some pride to a study of Washington's great act in crossing the Delaware, from a wax-work of great accuracy. The reader will avoid confusing Washington with the author, who is dressed in a plaid suit and on the shore, while Washington may be seen in this end of the boat with the air of one who has just discovered the location of a glue-factory on the side of the river.

A directory of Washington's head-quarters has been arranged by the author of this book, and at a reunion of the general's body-servants to be held in the future the work will be on sale.

The name of George Washington has always had about it a glamour that made him appear more in the light of a god than a tall man with large feet and a mouth made to fit an old-fashioned full-dress pumpkin pie.

George Washington's face has beamed out upon us for many years now, on postage-stamps and currency, in marble and plaster and in bronze, in photographs of original portraits, paintings, and stereoscopic views. We have seen him on horseback and on foot, on the war-path and on skates, playing the flute, cussing his troops for their shiftlessness, and then, in the solitude of the forest, with his snorting war-horse tied to a tree, engaged in prayer.

STUDY OF WASHINGTON CROSSING THE DELAWARE.

MY GREATEST WORK.

We have seen all these pictures of George, till we are led to believe that he did not breathe our air or eat American groceries. But George Washington was not perfect. I say this after a long and careful study of his life, and I do not say it to detract the very smallest iota from the proud history of the Father of his Country. I say it simply that the boys of America who want to become George Washingtons will not feel so timid about trying it.

When I say that George Washington, who now lies so calmly in the lime-kiln at Mount Vernon, could reprimand and reproach his subordinates, at times, in a way to make the ground crack open and break up the ice in the Delaware a week earlier than usual, I do not mention it in order to show the boys of our day that profanity will make them resemble George Washington. That was one of his weak points, and no doubt he was ashamed of it, as he ought to have been. Some poets think that if they get drunk and stay drunk they will resemble Edgar A. Poe and George D. Prentice. There are lawyers who play poker year after year and get regularly skinned because they have heard that some of the able lawyers of the past century used to come home at night with poker-chips in their pockets.

Whiskey will not make a poet, nor poker a great pleader. And yet I have seen poets who relied on the potency of their breath, and lawyers who knew more of the habits of a bobtail flush than they ever did of the statutes in such case made and provided.

George Washington was always ready. If you wanted a man to be first in war, you could call on George. If you desired an adult who would be first baseman in time of peace, Mr. Washington could be telephoned at any hour of the day or night. If you needed a man to be first in the hearts of his countrymen, George's post-office address was at once secured.

Though he was a great man, he was once a poor boy. How often you hear that in America! Here it is a positive disadvantage to be born wealthy. And yet sometimes I wish they had experimented a little that way on me. I do not ask now to be born rich, of course, because it is too late; but it seems to me that, with my natural good sense and keen insight into human nature, I could have struggled along under the burdens and cares of wealth with great success. I do not care to die wealthy, but if I could have been born wealthy it seems to me I would have been tickled almost to death.

WASHINGTON PLAYING THE FLUTE.

I love to believe that true greatness is not accidental. To think and to say that greatness is a lottery, is pernicious. Man may be wrong sometimes in his judgment of others, both individually and in the aggregate, but he who gets ready to be a great man will surely find the opportunity.

You will wonder whom I got to write this sentiment for me, but you will never find out.

THE AWKWARD SQUAD.

In conclusion, let me say that George Washington was successful for three reasons. One was that he never shook the confidence of his friends. Another was that he had a strong will without being a mule. Some people cannot distinguish between being firm and being a big blue donkey.

Another reason why Washington is loved and honored to-day is that he died before we had a chance to get tired of him. This is greatly superior to the method adopted by many modern statesmen, who wait till their constituency weary of them, and then reluctantly pass away.

N. B.—Since writing the foregoing I have found that Washington was not born a poor boy,—a discovery which redounds greatly to his credit,—that he was able to accomplish so much, and yet could get his weekly spending money and sport a French nurse in his extreme youth.

B. N.

CHAPTER XIII.

CONTRASTS WITH THE PRESENT DAY.

Here it may be well to speak briefly of the contrast between the usages and customs of the period preceding the Revolution, and the present day. Some of these customs and regulations have improved with the lapse of time, others undoubtedly have not.

Two millions of people constituted the entire number of whites, while away to the westward the red brother extended indefinitely. Religiously they were Protestants, and essentially they were 'a God-fearing people.' Taught to obey a power they were afraid of, they naturally turned with delight to the service of a God whose genius in the erection of a boundless and successful hell challenged their admiration and esteem. So, too, their own executions of Divine laws were successful as they gave pain, and the most beautiful features of Christianity,—namely, love and charity,—according to history, were not cultivated very much.

There were in New England at one time twelve offences punishable with death, and in Virginia seventeen. This would indicate that the death-penalty is getting unpopular very fast, and that in the contiguous future humane

THE TOWN WATCHMAN.

people will wonder why murder should have called for murder, in this brainy, charitable, and occult age, in which man seems almost able to pry open the future and catch a glimpse of Destiny underneath the great tent that has heretofore held him off by means of death's prohibitory rates.

In Hartford people had to get up when the town watchman rang his bell. The affairs of the family, and private matters too numerous to mention, were regulated by the selectmen. The catalogues of Harvard and Yale were regulated according to the standing of the family as per record in the old country, and not as per bust measurement and merit, as it is to-day.

Scolding women, however, were gagged and tied to their front doors, so that the populace could bite its thumb at them, and hired girls received fifty dollars a year, with the understanding that they were not to have over two days out each week, except Sunday and the days they had to go and see their 'sick sisters.'

Some cloth-weaving was indulged in, and homespun was the principal material used for clothing. Mrs. Washington had sixteen spinning-wheels in her house. Her husband often wore homespun while at home, and on rainy days sometimes placed a pair of home-made trousers of the barn-door variety in the Presidential chair.

Money was very scarce, and ammunition very valuable. In 1635 musket-balls passed for farthings, and to see a New England peasant making change with the red brother at thirty yards was a common and delightful scene.

The first press was set up in Cambridge in 1639, with the statement that it 'had come to stay.' Books printed in those days were mostly sermons filled with the most comfortable assurance that the man who let loose his intellect and allowed it to disbelieve some very difficult things would be essentially— —well, I hate to say right here in a book what would happen to him.

BOOKS FILLED WITH
ASSURANCES OF FUTURE
DAMNATION.

The first daily paper, called *The Federal Orrery*, was issued three hundred years after Columbus discovered America. It was not popular, and killed off the news-boys who tried to call it on the streets: so it perished.

There was a public library in New York, from which books were loaned at fourpence ha'penny per week. New York thus became very early the seat of learning, and soon afterwards began to abuse the site where Chicago now stands.

Travel was slow, the people went on horseback or afoot, and when they could go by boat it was regarded as a success. Wagons finally made the trip from New York to Philadelphia in the wild time of forty-eight hours, and the line was called The Flying Dutchman, or some other euphonious name. Benjamin Franklin, whose biography occurs in Chapter XV., was then Postmaster-General.

He was the first bald-headed man of any prominence in the history of America. He and his daughter Sally took a trip in a chaise, looking over the entire system, and going to all offices. Nothing pleased the Postmaster-General like quietly slipping into a place like Sandy Bottom and catching the postmaster reading over the postal cards and committing them to memory.

Calfskin shoes up to the Revolution were the exclusive property of the gentry, and the rest wore cowhide and were extremely glad to mend them themselves. These were greased every week with tallow, and could be worn on either foot with impunity. Rights and lefts were never thought of until after the Revolutionary War, but to-day the American shoe is the most symmetrical, comfortable, and satisfactory shoe made in the world. The British shoe is said to be more comfortable. Possibly for a British foot it is so, but for a foot containing no breathing-apparatus or viscera it is somewhat roomy and clumsy.

CAUGHT BY FRANKLIN READING POSTAL CARDS.

Farmers and laborers of those days wore green or red baize in the shape of jackets, and their breeches were made of leather or bedticking. Our ancestors dressed plainly, and a man who could not make over two hundred pounds per year was prohibited from dressing up or wearing lace worth over two shillings per yard. It was a pretty sad time for literary men, as they were thus compelled to wear clothing like the common laborers.

Lord Cornwallis once asked his aidy kong why the American poet always had such an air of listening as if for some expected sound. 'I give it up,' retorted the aidy kong. 'It is,' said Lord Cornwallis, as he took a large drink from a jug which he had tied to his saddle, 'because he is trying to see if he cannot hear his bed-ticking.' On the following day he surrendered his army, and went home to spring his *bon-mot* on George III.

Yet the laws were very stringent in other respects besides apparel. A man was publicly whipped for killing a fowl on the Sabbath in New England. In order to keep a tavern and sell rum, one had to be of good moral character and possess property, which was a good thing. The names of drunkards were posted up in the alehouses, and the keepers forbidden to sell them liquor. No person under twenty years of age could use tobacco in Connecticut without a physician's order, and no one was allowed to use it more than once a day, and then not within ten miles of any house. It was a common thing to see large picnic-parties going out into the backwoods of Connecticut to smoke.

(Will the reader excuse me a moment while I light up a peculiarly black and redolent pipe?)

Only the gentry were called Mr. and Mrs. This included the preacher and his wife. A friend of mine who is one of the gentry of this century got on the trail of his ancestry last spring, and traced them back to where they were not allowed to be called Mr. and Mrs., and, fearing he would fetch up in Scotland Yard if he kept on, he slowly unrolled the bottoms of his trousers, got a job on the railroad, and since then his friends are gradually returning to him. He is well pleased now, and looks humbly gratified even if you call him a gent.

LORD CORNWALLIS'S CONUNDRUM.

The Scriptures were literally interpreted, and the Old Testament was read every morning, even if the ladies fainted.

The custom yet noticed sometimes in country churches and festive gatherings of placing the males and females on opposite sides of the room was originated not so much as a punishment to both, as to give the men an opportunity to act together when the red brother felt ill at ease.

I am glad the red brother does not molest us nowadays, and make us sit apart that way. Keep away, red brother; remain on your reservation, please, so that the pale-face may sit by the loved one and hold her little soft hand during the sermon.

Church services meant business in those days. People brought their dinners and had a general penitential gorge. Instrumental music was proscribed, as per Amos fifth chapter and twenty-third verse, and the length of prayer was measured by the physical endurance of the performer.

The preacher often boiled his sermon down to four hours, and the sexton up-ended the hourglass each hour. Boys who went to sleep in church were sand-bagged, and grew up to be border murderers.

New York people were essentially Dutch. New York gets her Santa Claus, her doughnuts, crullers, cookies, and many of her odors, from the Dutch. The New York matron ran to fine linen and a polished door-knocker, while the New England housewife spun linsey-woolsey and knit 'yarn mittens' for those she loved.

Philadelphia was the largest city in the United States, and was noted for its cleanliness and generally sterling qualities of mind and heart, its Sabbath trance and clean white door-steps.

The Southern Colonies were quite different from those of the North. In place of thickly-settled towns there were large plantations with African villages near the house of the owner. The proprietor was a sort of country squire, living in considerable comfort for those days. He fed and clothed everybody, black or white, who lived on the estate, and waited patiently for the colored people to do his work and keep well, so that they would be more valuable. The colored people were blessed with children at a great rate, so that at this writing, though voteless, they send a large number of members to Congress. This cheers the Southern heart and partially recoups him for his chickens. (See Appendix.)

The South then, as now, cured immense quantities of tobacco, while the North tried to cure those who used it.

Washington was a Virginian. He packed his own flour with his own hands, and it was never inspected. People who knew him said that the only man who ever tried to inspect Washington's flour was buried under a hill of choice watermelons at Mount Vernon.

Along the James and Rappahannock the vast estates often passed from father to son according to the law of entail, and such a thing as a poor man 'prior to the war' must have been unknown.

NOT RICH BEFORE THE WAR.

Education, however, flourished more at the North, owing partly to the fact that the people lived more in communities. Governor Berkeley of Virginia was opposed to free schools from the start, and said, 'I thank God there are no free schools nor printing-presses here, and I hope we shall not have them these hundred years.' His prayer has been answered.

CHAPTER XIV.

THE REVOLUTIONARY WAR.

William Pitt was partly to blame for the Revolutionary War. He claimed that the Colonists ought not to manufacture so much as a horseshoe nail except by permission of Parliament.

It was already hard enough to be a colonist, without the privilege of expressing one's self even to an Indian without being fined. But when we pause to think that England seemed to demand that the colonist should take the long wet walk to Liverpool during a busy season of the year to get his horse shod, we say at once that P. Henry was right when he exclaimed that the war was inevitable and moved that permission be granted for it to come.

Then came the Stamp Act, making almost everything illegal that was not written on stamp paper furnished by the maternal country.

John Adams, Patrick Henry, and John Otis made speeches regarding the situation. Bells were tolled, and fasting and prayer marked the first of November, the day for the law to go into effect.

These things alarmed England for the time, and the Stamp Act was repealed; but the king, who had been pretty free with his money and had entertained a good deal, began to look out for a chance to tax the Colonists, and ordered his Exchequer Board to attend to it.

Patrick Henry got excited, and said in an early speech, 'Cæsar had his Brutus,

PATRICK HENRY.

Charles the First his Cromwell, and George the Third — —' Here he paused and took a long swig of pure water, and added, looking at the newspaper reporters, 'If this be treason, make the most of it.' He also said that George the Third might profit by their example. A good many would like to know what he started out to say, but it is too hard to determine.

Boston ladies gave up tea and used the dried leaves of the raspberry, and the girls of 1777 graduated in homespun. Could the iron heel of despotism crunch such a spirit of liberty as that? Scarcely. In one family at Newport four hundred and eighty-seven yards of cloth and thirty-six pairs of stockings were spun and made in eighteen months.

When the war broke out it is estimated that each Colonial soldier had twenty-seven pairs of blue woollen socks with white double heels and toes. Does the intelligent reader believe that 'Tommy Atkins,' with two pairs of socks 'and hit a-rainin',' could whip men with twenty-seven pairs each? Not without restoratives.

Troops were now sent to restore order. They were clothed by the British government, but boarded around with the Colonists. This was irritating to the people, because they had never met or called on the British troops. Again, they did not know the troops were coming, and had made no provision for them.

Boston was considered the hot-bed of the rebellion, and General Gage was ordered to send two regiments of troops there. He did so, and a fight ensued, in which three citizens were killed.

In looking over this incident, we must not forget that in those days three citizens went a good deal farther than they do now.

The fight, however, was brief. General Gage, getting into a side street, separated from his command, and, coming out on the Common abruptly, he tried eight or nine more streets, but he came out each time on the Common, until, torn with conflicting emotions, he hired a Herdic, which took him around the corner to his quarters.

THE BRITISH BOARDING 'ROUND.

On December 16, 1773, occurred the tea-party at Boston, which must have been a good deal livelier than those of to-day. The historian regrets that he was not there; he would have tried to be the life of the party.

England had finally so arranged the price of tea that, including the tax, it was cheaper in America than in the old country. This exasperated the patriots, who claimed that they were confronted by a theory and not a condition. At Charleston this tea was stored in damp cellars, where it spoiled. New York and Philadelphia returned their ships, but the British would not allow any shenanegin', as George III. so tersely termed it, in Boston.

Therefore a large party met in Faneuil Hall and decided that the tea should not be landed. A party made up as Indians, and, going on board, threw the tea overboard. Boston Harbor, as far out as the Bug Light, even to-day, is said to be carpeted with tea-grounds.

George III. now closed Boston harbor and made General Gage Governor of Massachusetts. The Virginia Assembly murmured at this, and was dissolved and sent home without its mileage.

BOSTON TEA-PARTY, 1773.

Those opposed to royalty were termed Whigs, those in favor were called Tories. Now they are called Chappies or Authors.

On the 5th of September, 1774, the first Continental Congress assembled at Philadelphia and was entertained by the Clover Club. Congress acted slowly even then, and after considerable delay resolved that the conduct of Great Britain was, under the circumstances, uncalled for. It also voted to hold no intercourse with Great Britain, and decided not to visit Shakespeare's grave unless the mother-country should apologize.

In 1775, on the 19th of April, General Gage sent out troops to see about some military stores at Concord, but at Lexington he met with a company of minute-men gathering on the village green. Major Pitcairn, who was in command of the Tommies, rode up to the minute-men, and, drawing his bright new Sheffield sword, exclaimed, 'Disperse, you rebels! throw down your arms and disperse!' or some such remark as that.

BOSTON TEA PARTY, 1893.

The Americans hated to do that, so they did not. In the skirmish that ensued, seven of their number were killed.

Thus opened the Revolutionary War,—a contest which but for the earnestness and irritability of the Americans would have been extremely brief. It showed the relative difference between the fighting qualities of soldiers who fight for two pounds ten shillings per month and those who fight because they have lost their temper.

The regulars destroyed the stores, but on the way home they found every rock-pile hid an old-fashioned gun and minute-man. This shows that there must have been an enormous number of minute-men then. All the English who got back to Boston were those who went out to reinforce the original command.

The news went over the country like wildfire. These are the words of the historian. Really, that is a poor comparison, for wildfire doesn't jump rivers and bays, or get up and eat breakfast by candle-light in order to be on the road and spread the news.

General Putnam left a pair of tired steers standing in the furrow, and rode one hundred miles without feed or water to Boston.

Twenty thousand men were soon at work building intrenchments around Boston, so that the English troops could not get out to the suburbs where many of them resided.

GENERAL PUTNAM LEAVING A PAIR OF TIRED STEERS.

I will now speak of the battle of Bunker Hill.

This battle occurred June 17. The Americans heard that their enemy intended to fortify Bunker Hill, and so they determined to do it themselves, in order to have it done in a way that would be a credit to the town.

A body of men under Colonel Prescott, after prayer by the President of Harvard University, marched to Charlestown Neck. They decided to fortify Breed's Hill, as it was more commanding, and all night long they kept on fortifying. The surprise of the English at daylight was well worth going from Lowell to witness.

Howe sent three thousand men across and formed them on the landing. He marched them up the hill to within ten rods of the earthworks, when it occurred to Prescott that it would now be the appropriate thing to fire. He made a statement of that kind to his troops, and those of the enemy who were alive went back to Charlestown. But that was no place for them, as they had previously set it afire, so they came back up the hill, where they were once more well received and tendered the freedom of a future state.

GENERAL HOWE'S SUGGESTION.

Three times the English did this, when the ammunition in the fortifications gave out, and they charged with fixed bayonets and reinforcements.

The Americans were driven from the field, but it was a victory after all. It united the Colonies and made them so vexed at the English that it took some time to bring on an era of good feeling.

Lord Howe, referring afterwards to this battle, said that the Americans did not stand up and fight like the regulars, suggesting that thereafter the Colonial army should arrange itself in the following manner before a battle!

However, the suggestion was not acted on. The Colonial soldiers declined to put on a bright red coat and a pill-box cap, that kept falling off in battle, thus delaying the carnage, but preferred to wear homespun which was of a neutral shade, and shoot their enemy from behind stumps. They said it was all right to dress up for a muster, but they preferred their working-clothes for fighting. After the war a statistician made the estimate that nine per cent. of the

British troops were shot while ascertaining if their caps were on straight.[4]

PUTNAM'S FLIGHT.

General Israel Putnam was known as the champion rough rider of his day, and once when hotly pursued rode down three flights of steps, which, added to the flight he made from the English soldiers, made four flights. Putnam knew not fear or cowardice, and his name even to-day is the synonyme for valor and heroism.

FRANKLIN'S MORNING HUNT FOR HIS SHOES.

CHAPTER XV.

BENJAMIN FRANKLIN, LL.D., PH.G., F.R.S., ETC.

It is considered advisable by the historian at this time to say a word regarding Dr. Franklin, our fellow-townsman, and a journalist who was the Charles A. Dana of his time.

Franklin's memory will remain green when the names of the millionaires of to-day are forgotten. Coextensive with the name of E.

Rosewater of the *Omaha Bee* we will find that of Benjamin Franklin, whose bust sits above the fireplace of the writer at this moment, while a large Etruscan hornet is making a phrenological examination of same.

But let us proceed to more fully mark out the life and labors of this remarkable man.

Benjamin Franklin, formerly of Boston, came very near being an only child. If seventeen children had not come to bless the home of Benjamin's parents they would have been childless. Think of getting up in the morning and picking out your shoes and stockings from among seventeen pairs of them!

THE PRINTER'S TOWEL.

Imagine yourself a child, gentle reader, in a family where you would be called upon every morning to select your own cud of spruce gum from a collection of seventeen similar cuds stuck on a window-sill! And yet Benjamin Franklin never murmured or repined. He desired to go to sea, and to avoid this he was apprenticed to his brother James, who was a printer.

It is said that Franklin at once took hold of the great Archimedean

lever, and jerked it early and late in the interests of freedom.

It is claimed that Franklin, at this time, invented the deadly weapon known as the printer's towel. He found that a common crash towel could be saturated with glue, molasses, antimony, concentrated lye, and roller-composition, and that after a few years of time and perspiration it would harden so that 'A Constant Reader' or 'Veritas' could be stabbed with it and die soon.

Many believe that Franklin's other scientific experiments were productive of more lasting benefit to mankind than this, but I do not agree with them.

FRANKLIN AS FOREMAN.

His paper was called the *New England Courant*. It was edited jointly by James and Benjamin Franklin, and was started to supply a long-felt want.

Benjamin edited it a part of the time, and James a part of the time. The idea of having two editors was not for the purpose of giving volume to the editorial page, but it was necessary for one to run the paper while the other was in jail.

In those days you could not sass the king, and then, when the king came in the office the next day and stopped his paper and took out his ad., put it off on 'our informant' and go right along with the paper. You had to go to jail, while your subscribers wondered why their paper did not come, and the paste soured in the tin dippers in the sanctum, and the circus passed by on the other side.

FRANKLIN EXPERIMENTING WITH LIGHTNING.

How many of us to-day, fellow-journalists, would be willing to stay in jail while the lawn festival and the kangaroo came and went? Who of all our company would go to a prison-cell for the cause of freedom while a double-column ad. of sixteen aggregated circuses, and eleven congresses of ferocious beasts, fierce and fragrant from their native lair, went by us?

At the age of seventeen Ben got disgusted with his brother, and went to Philadelphia and New York, where he got a chance to 'sub' for a few weeks and then got a regular 'sit.'

Franklin was a good printer, and finally got to be a foreman. He made an excellent foreman, sitting by the hour in the composing-room and spitting on the stove, while he cussed the make-up and press-work of the other papers. Then he would go into the editorial rooms and scare the editors to death with a wild shriek for more copy.

He knew just how to conduct himself as a foreman so that strangers would think he owned the paper.

In 1730, at the age of twenty-four, Franklin married, and established the *Pennsylvania Gazette*. He was then regarded as a great man, and almost every one took his paper.

Franklin grew to be a great journalist, and spelled hard words with great fluency. He never tried to be a humorist in any of his newspaper work, and everybody respected him.

Along about 1746 he began to study the habits and construction of lightning, and inserted a local in his paper in which he said that he would be obliged to any of his readers who might notice any new or odd specimens of lightning, if they would send them in to the *Gazette* office for examination.

Every time there was a thunderstorm Franklin would tell the foreman to edit the paper, and, armed with a string and an old door-key, he would go out on the hills and get enough lightning for a mess.

FRANKLIN VISITING GEORGE III.

In 1753 Franklin was made postmaster of the Colonies. He made a good Postmaster-General, and people say there were fewer mistakes in distributing their mail then than there have ever been since. If a man mailed a letter in those days, old Ben Franklin saw that it went to where it was addressed.

Franklin frequently went over to England in those days, partly on business and partly to shock the king. He liked to go to the castle with his breeches tucked in his boots, figuratively speaking, and attract a great deal of attention.

FRANKLIN ENTERING PHILADELPHIA.

It looked odd to the English, of course, to see him come into the royal presence, and, leaning his wet umbrella up against the throne, ask the king, 'How's trade?'

Franklin never put on any frills, but he was not afraid of a crowned head. He used to say, frequently, that a king to him was no more than a seven-spot.

He did his best to prevent the Revolutionary War, but he couldn't do it. Patrick Henry had said that the war was inevitable, and had given it permission to come, and it came.

He also went to Paris, and got acquainted with a few crowned heads there. They thought a good deal of him in Paris, and offered him a corner lot if he would build there and start a paper. They also promised him the county printing; but he said, No, he would have to go back to America or his wife might get uneasy about him. Franklin wrote 'Poor Richard's Almanac' in 1732 to 1757, and it was republished in England.

Franklin little thought, when he went to the throne-room in his leather riding-clothes and hung his hat on the throne, that he was inaugurating a custom of wearing groom clothes which would in these days be so popular among the English.

Dr. Franklin entered Philadelphia eating a loaf of bread and carrying a loaf under each arm, passing beneath the window of the girl to whom he afterwards gave his hand in marriage.

Nearly everybody in America, except Dr. Mary Walker, was once a poor boy.

CHAPTER XVI.

THE CRITICAL PERIOD.

Ethan Allen and Benedict Arnold on the 10th of May led two small companies to Ticonderoga, a strong fortress tremendously fortified, and with its name also across the front door. Ethan Allen, a brave Vermonter born in Connecticut, entered the sally-port, and was shot at by a guard whose musket failed to report. Allen entered and demanded the surrender of the fortress.

'By whose authority?' asked the commandant.

'By the authority of the Great Jehovah and the Continental Congress,' said Allen, brandishing his naked sword at a great rate.

'Very well,' said the officer: 'if you put it on those grounds, all right, if you will excuse the appearance of things. We were just cleaning up, and everything is by the heels here.'

'Never mind,' said Allen, who was the soul of politeness. 'We put on no frills at home, and so we are ready to take things as we find them.'

The Americans therefore got a large amount of munitions of war, both here and at Crown Point.

General Washington was now appointed commander-in-chief of all the troops at the second session of the Continental Congress. On his arrival at Boston there were only fourteen thousand men. He took command under the historic elm at Cambridge. He was dressed in a blue broadcloth coat with flaps and revers of same, trimmed with large beautiful buttons. He also wore buff small-clothes, with openings at the sides where pockets are now put in, but at that time given up to space. They were made in such a way as to prevent the naked eye from discovering at once whether he was in advance or retreat. He also wore silk stockings and a cocked hat.

The lines of Dryden starting off 'Mark his majestic fabric' were suggested by his appearance and general style. He always dressed well and rode a good horse, but at Valley Forge frosted his feet severely, and could have drawn a pension, 'but no,' said he, 'I can still work at light employment, like being President, and so I will not ask for a pension.'

Each soldier had less than nine cartridges, but Washington managed to keep General Gage penned up in Boston, and, as Gage knew very few people there, it was a dull winter for him.

The boys of Boston had built snow hills on the Common, and used to slide down them to the ice below, but the British soldiers tore down their coasting-places and broke up the ice on the pond.

They stood it a long time, rebuilding their playground as often as it was torn down, until the spirit of American freedom could endure it no longer. They then organized a committee consisting of eight boys who were noted for their great philosophical research, and with Charles Sumner Muzzy, the eloquent savant from Milk Street, as chairman, the committee started for General Gage's head-quarters, to confer with him regarding the matter.

In the picture Mr. Muzzy is seen addressing General Gage. The boy in the centre with the colored glasses is Marco Bozzaris Cobb, who discovered and first brought into use the idea of putting New Orleans molasses into Boston brown bread. To the left of Mr. Cobb is Mr. Jehoab Nye, who afterwards became the Rev. Jehoab Nye and worked with heart and voice for over eight of the best years of his life against the immorality of the codfish-ball, before he learned of its true relations towards society.

Above and between these two stands Whomsoever J. Opper, who wrote 'How to make the Garden Pay' and 'What Responsible Person will see that my Grave is kept green?' In the background we see the tall form of Wherewithal G. Lumpy, who introduced the Pompadour hair-cut into Massachusetts and grew up to be a great man with enlarged joints but restricted ideas.

INTELLECTUAL TRIUMPH OF THE YOUTH OF BOSTON OVER
GENERAL GAGE.

Charles Sumner Muzzy addressed General Gage at some length,
somewhat to the surprise of Gage, who admitted in a few well-
chosen words that the committee was right, and that if he had his
way about it there should be no more trouble.

Charles was followed by Marco Bozzaris Cobb, who spoke briefly of
the boon of liberty, closing as follows: 'We point with pride, sir, to
the love of freedom, which is about the only excitement we have. We
love our country, sir, whether we love anything else much or not.
The distant wanderer of American birth, sir, pines for his country.
'Oh, give me back,' he goes on to say, 'my own fair land across the
bright blue sea, the land of beauty and of worth, the bright land of
the free, where tyrant foot hath never trod, nor bigot forged a chain.
Oh, would that I were safely back in that bright land again!''

Mr. Wherewithal G. Lumpy said he had hardly expected to be called
upon, and so had not prepared himself, but this occasion forcibly
brought to his mind the words also of the poet, 'Our country stands,'
said he, 'with outstretched hands appealing to her boys; from them
must flow her weal or woe, her anguish or her joys. A ship she rides
on human tides which rise and sink anon: each giant wave may

prove her grave, or bear her nobly on. The friends of right, with armor bright, a valiant Christian band, through God her aid may yet be made, a blessing to our land.'

GENERAL GAGE THINKING IT OVER.

General Gage was completely overcome, and asked for a moment to go apart and think it over, which he did, returning with an air which reminded one of 'Ten Nights in a Bar-Room.'

'You may go, my brave boys; and be assured that if my troops molest you in the future, or anywhere else, I will overpower them and strew the Common with their corses.

'Of corse he will,' said the hairy boy to the right of Whomsoever J. Opper, who afterwards became the father of a lad who grew up to be editor of the Persiflage column of the *Atlantic Monthly*.

Thus the boys of America impressed General Gage with their courage and patriotism and grew up to be good men.

LORD HOWE FELT THE COLD VERY KEENLY.

An expedition to Canada was fitted out the same winter, and an attack made on Quebec, in which General Montgomery was killed and Benedict Arnold showed that he was a brave soldier, no matter how the historian may have hopped on him afterwards.

The Americans should not have tried to take Canada. Canada was, as Henry Clay once said, a persimmon a trifle too high for the American pole, and it is the belief of the historian, whose tears have often wet the pages of this record, that in the future Canada will be what America is now, a free country with a national debt of her own, a flag of her own, an executive of her own, and a regular annual crisis of her own, like other nations.

In 1776 Boston was evacuated. Washington, in order to ascertain whether Lord Howe had a call to fish, cut bait, or go ashore, began to fortify Dorchester Heights, March 17, and on the following morning he was not a little surprised to note the change. As the weather was raw, and he had been in-doors a good deal during the winter, Lord Howe felt the cold very keenly. He went to the window and looked at the Americans, but he would come back chilly and ill-tempered to the fire each time. Finally he hitched up and went away to Halifax, where he had acquaintances.

On June 28 an attack was made by the English on Fort Moultrie. It was built of palmetto logs, which are said to be the best thing in the world to shoot into if one wishes to recover the balls and use them again. Palmetto logs accept and retain balls for many years, and are therefore good for forts.

When the fleet got close enough to the fort so that the brave Charlestonians could see the expression on the admiral's face, they turned loose with everything they had, grape, canister, solid shot, chain-shot, bar-shot, stove-lids, muffin-irons, newspaper cuts, etc., etc., so that the decks were swept of every living thing except the admiral.

JEFFERSON DICTATING THE DECLARATION OF
INDEPENDENCE.

General Clinton by land tried to draw the attention of the rear gunners of the fort, but he was a poor draughtsman, and so retired, and both the land and naval forces quit Charleston and went to New York, where board was not so high.

```
                        700 Market Street.
Telephone No. 15.790.
                              Philadelphia,  July 4, 1776.
(Dictated.)                              A.  Folio 32.
              DECLARATION OF INDEPENDENCE.
      When, in thecourse of human eventss, it becomes necessary
for a one peopletodissolve the political bandswwhich have connected
them with themamother,xand to assume, among the powers of the earth,
the separate and the equalstation to which the laws of nature and of
nature's God entitlethem, a decent respect and to the opinions of the
mankind requires that they should declare the causes which impel them
to theseparations.
```

FAC-SIMILE OF DICTATION.

July 4 was deemed a good time to write a Declaration of Independence and have it read in the grove.

Richard Henry Lee, of Virginia, moved that 'the United Colonies are, and of right ought to be, free and Independent states.' John Adams, of Massachusetts, seconded the resolution. This was passed July 2, and the report of the committee appointed to draw up a Declaration of Independence was adopted July 4.

The Declaration was dictated by Thomas Jefferson, who wrote the most melodious English of any American of his time.

Jefferson had a vocabulary next to Noah Webster, with all the dramatic power of Dan. He composed the piece one evening after his other work. We give a facsimile of the opening lines.

Philadelphia was a scene of great excitement. The streets were thronged, and people sat down on the nice clean door-steps with perfect recklessness, although the steps had just been cleaned with ammonia and wiped off with a chamois-skin. It was a day long to be remembered, and one that made George III. wish that he had reconsidered his birth.

RINGING THE
LIBERTY BELL.

In the steeple of the old State-House was a bell which had fortunately upon it the line 'Proclaim liberty throughout all the land unto all the inhabitants thereof.' It was rung by the old man in charge, though he had lacked faith up to that moment in Congress. He believed that Congress would not pass the resolution and adopt the Declaration till after election.

Thus was the era of good feeling inaugurated both North and South. There was no North then, no South, no East, no West; just one common country, with Washington acting as father of same. Oh, how nice it must have been!

Washington was one of the sweetest men in the United States. He gave his hand in marriage to a widow woman who had two children and a dark red farm in Virginia.

CHAPTER XVII.

THE BEGINNING OF THE END.

The British army now numbered thirty thousand troops, while Washington's entire command was not over seven thousand strong. The Howes, one a general and the other an admiral, now turned their attention to New York. Washington, however, was on the ground beforehand.

Howe's idea was to first capture Brooklyn, so that he could have a place in which to sleep at nights while engaged in taking New York.

The battle was brief. Howe attacked the little army in front, while General Clinton got around by a circuitous route to the rear of the Colonial troops and cut them off. The Americans lost one thousand men by death or capture. The prisoners were confined in the old sugar-house on Liberty Street, where they suffered the most miserable and indescribable deaths.

The army of the Americans fortunately escaped by Fulton Ferry in a fog, otherwise it would have been obliterated. Washington now fortified Harlem Heights, and later withdrew to White Plains. Afterwards he retired to a fortified camp called North Castle.

Howe feared to attack him there, and so sent the Hessians, who captured Fort Washington, November 16.

It looked scaly for the Americans, as Motley says, and Philadelphia bade fair to join New York and other cities held by the British. The English van could be seen from the Colonial rear column. The American troops were almost barefooted, and left their blood-stained tracks on the frozen road.

NYE AS THE
DUKE OF SANDY BOTTOM.

It was at this time that Washington crossed the Delaware and thereby found himself on the other side; while Howe decided to remain, as the river was freezing, and when the ice got strong enough, cross over and kill the Americans at his leisure. Had he followed the Colonial army, it is quite sure now that the English would have conquered, and the author would have been the Duke of Sandy Bottom, instead of a plain American citizen, unknown, unhonored, and unsung.

Washington decided that he must strike a daring blow while his troops had any hope or vitality left; and so on Christmas night, after crossing the Delaware as shown elsewhere, he fell on the Hessians at Trenton in the midst of their festivities, captured one thousand prisoners, and slew the leader.

The Hessians were having a symposium at the time, and though the commander received an important note of warning during the Christmas dinner, he thrust it into his pocket and bade joy be unconfined.

When daylight came, the Hessians were mostly moving in alcoholic circles trying to find their guns. Washington lost only four men, and two of those were frozen to death.

The result of this fight gave the Colonists courage and taught them at the same time that it would be best to avoid New Jersey symposiums till after the war was over.

Having made such a hit in crossing the Delaware, Washington decided to repeat the performance on the 3d of January. He was attacked at Trenton by Cornwallis, who is known in history for his justly celebrated surrender. He waited till morning, having been repulsed at sundown. Washington left his camp-fires burning, surrounded the British, captured two hundred prisoners, and got away to Morristown Heights in safety. If the ground had not frozen, General Washington could not have moved his forty cannon; but, fortunately, the thermometer was again on his side, and he never lost a gun.

September 11 the English got into the Chesapeake, and Washington announced in the papers that he would now fight the battle of the Brandywine, which he did.

THE COLONIAL SURPRISE-PARTY AT TRENTON.

Marie Jean Paul Roch Yves Gilbert Motier, Marquis de La Fayette, fought bravely with the Americans in this battle, twice having his name shot from under him.

The patriots were routed, scoring a goose-egg and losing Philadelphia.

October 4, Washington attacked the enemy at Germantown, and was beaten back just as victory was arranging to perch on his banner. Poor Washington now retired to Valley Forge, where he put in about the dullest winter of his life.

The English had not been so successful in the North. At first the Americans could only delay Burgoyne by felling trees in the path of his eight thousand men, which is a very unsatisfactory sort of warfare, but at last Schuyler, who had borne the burden and heat of the day, was succeeded by Gates, and good luck seemed to come slowly his way.

A foolish boy with bullet-holes cut in his clothes ran into St. Leger's troops, and out of breath told them to turn back or they would fill a drunkard's grave. Officers asked him about the numbers of the enemy, and he pointed to the leaves of the trees, shrieked, and ran for his life. He ran several days, and was barely able to keep ahead of St. Leger's troops by a neck.

Burgoyne at another time sent a detachment under Colonel Baum to take the stores at Bennington, Vermont. He was met by General Stark and the militia. Stark said, 'Here come the redcoats, and we must beat them to-day, or Molly Stark is a widow.' This neat little remark made an instantaneous hit, and when they counted up their string of prisoners at night they found they had six hundred souls and a Hessian.

Burgoyne now felt blue and unhappy. Besides, his troops were covered with wood-ticks and had had no washing done for three weeks.

He moved southward and attacked Gates at Bemis Heights, or, as a British wit had it, 'gave Gates ajar,' near Saratoga. A wavering fight occupied the day, and then both armies turned in and fortified for two weeks. Burgoyne saw that he was running out of food, and so was first to open fire.

Arnold, who had been deprived of his command since the last battle, probably to prevent his wiping out the entire enemy and getting promoted, was so maddened by the conflict that he dashed in before Gates could put him in the guard-house, and at the head of his old command, and without authority or hat, led the attack. Gates did not dare to come where Arnold was, to order him back, for it was a very warm place where Arnold was at the time. The enemy was thus driven to camp.

Arnold was shot in the same leg that was wounded at Quebec; so he was borne back to the extreme rear, where he found Gates eating a doughnut and speaking disrespectfully of Arnold.

A council was now held in Burgoyne's tent, and on the question of renewing the fight stood six to six, when an eighteen-pound hot shot went through the tent, knocking a stylographic pen out of General Burgoyne's hand. Almost at once he decided to surrender, and the entire army of six thousand men was surrendered, together with arms, portable bath-tubs, and leather hat-boxes. The Americans marched into their camp to the tune of Yankee Doodle, which is one of the most impudent compositions ever composed.

KNOCKING A STYLOGRAPHIC PEN OUT OF BURGOYNE'S HAND.

During the Valley Forge winter (1777-78) Continental currency depreciated in value so that an officer's pay would not buy his clothes. Many, having also spent their private funds for the prosecution of the war, were obliged to resign and hire out in the lumber woods in order to get food for their families. Troops had no blankets, and straw was not to be had. It was extremely sad; but there was no wavering. Officers were approached by the enemy with from one hundred to one thousand pounds if they would accept and use their influence to effect a reconciliation; but, with blazing eye and unfaltering attitude, each stated that he was not for sale, and returned to his frozen mud-hole to rest and dream of food and freedom.

Those were the untitled nobility from whom we sprung. Let us look over our personal record and see if we are living lives that are worthy of such heroic sires.

Five minutes will now be given the reader to make a careful examination of his personal record.

*   *   *   *   *   *

*   *   *   *   *   *

In the spring the joyful news came across the sea that, through the efforts of Benjamin Franklin, France had acknowledged the independence of the United States, and a fleet was on the way to assist the struggling troops.

The battle of Monmouth occurred June 28. Clinton succeeded Howe, and, alarmed by the news of the French fleet, the government ordered Clinton to concentrate his troops near New York, where there were better facilities for getting home.

Washington followed the enemy across New Jersey, overtaking them at Monmouth. Lee was in command, and got his men tangled in a swamp where the mosquitoes were quite plenty, and, losing courage, ordered a retreat.

Washington arrived at that moment, and bitterly upbraided Lee. He used the Flanders method of upbraiding, it is said, and Lee could not stand it. He started towards the enemy in preference to being there with Washington, who was still rebuking him. The fight was renewed, and all day long they fought. When night came, Clinton took his troops with him and went away where they could be by themselves.

An effort was made to get up a fight between the French fleet and the English at Newport for the championship, but a severe storm came up and prevented it.

In July the Wyoming Massacre, under the management of the Tories and Indians, commanded by Butler, took place in that beautiful valley near Wilkes Barre, Pennsylvania.

This massacre did more to make the Indians and Tories unpopular in this country than any other act of the war. The men were away in the army, and the women, children, and old men alone were left to the vengeance of the two varieties of savage. The Indians had never had gospel privileges, but the Tories had. Otherwise they resembled each other.

In 1779 the English seemed to have Georgia and the South pretty well to themselves. Prevost, the English general, made an attack on Charleston, but, learning that Lincoln was after him, decided that, as he had a telegram to meet a personal friend at Savannah, he would go there. In September, Lincoln, assisted by the French under D'Estaing, attacked Savannah. One thousand lives were lost, and D'Estaing showed the white feather to advantage. Count Pulaski lost his life in this fight. He was a brave Polish patriot, and his body was buried in the Savannah River.

The capture of Stony Point about this time by 'Mad Anthony Wayne' was one of the most brilliant battles of the war.

THE ONLY THING WAYNE WAS AFRAID OF.

Learning the countersign from a negro who sold strawberries to the British, the troops passed the guard over the bridge that covered the marsh, and, gagging the worthy inside guard, they marched up the hill with fixed bayonets and fixed the enemy to the number of six hundred.

The countersign was, 'The fort is won,' and so it was, in less time than it takes to ejaculate the word 'scat!' Wayne was wounded at the outset, but was carried up the hill in command, with a bandage tied about his head. He was a brave man, and never knew in battle what fear was. Yet, strange to say, a bat in his bed would make him start up and turn pale.

CHAPTER XVIII.

THE CLOSE OF THE REVOLUTION.

The atrocities introduced into this country by the Tories and Indians caused General Sullivan to go out against the measly enemy, whip him near Elmira, and destroy the fields of corn and villages in the Genesee country, where the Indian women were engaged in farming while their men-folks attended to the massacre industry.

GENERAL GATES'S PROPER CAREER.

The weak point with the Americans seemed to be lack of a suitable navy. A navy costs money, and the Colonists were poor. In 1775 they fitted out several swift sailing-vessels, which did good service. Inside of five years they captured over five hundred ships, cruised among the British isles, and it is reported that they captured war-vessels that were tied to the English wharves.

Paul Jones had a method of running his vessel alongside the enemy's, lashing the two together, and then having it out with the crew, generally winning in a canter. His idea in lashing the two ships together was to have one good ship to ride home on. Generally it was the one he captured, while his own, which was rotten, was allowed to go down. This was especially the case in the fight between the Richard and the Serapis, September 23, 1779.

In 1780 the war was renewed in South Carolina. Charleston, after a forty days' siege, was forced to surrender. Gates now took charge of the South, and also gave a sprinting exhibition at Camden, where he was almost wiped off the face of the earth. He had only two troops left at the close of the battle, and they could not keep up with Gates in the retreat. This battle and the retreat overheated Gates and sowed the seeds of heart-disease, from which he never recovered. He should have chosen a more peaceful life, such as the hen-traffic, or the growth of asparagus for the market.

Benedict Arnold has been severely reproached in history, but he was a brave soldier, and possibly serving under Gates, who jealously kept him in the background, had a good deal to do with the little European dicker which so darkened his brilliant career as a soldier.

ARNOLD'S RECEPTION IN ENGLAND.

Unhappy man! He was not well received in England, and, though a brilliant man, was forced to sit in a corner evening after evening and hear the English tell his humorous stories as their own.

The Carolinas were full of Tories, and opposition to English rule was practically abandoned in the South for the time, with the exception of that made in a desultory swamp-warfare by the partisan bands with such leaders as Marion, Sumter, and Pickens.

Two hundred thousand dollars of Continental money was the sum now out. Forty dollars of it would buy one dollar's worth of groceries; but the grocer had to know the customer pretty well, and even then it was more to accommodate than anything else that he sold at that price.

The British flooded the country with a counterfeit that was rather better-looking than the genuine: so that by the time a man had paid six hundred dollars for a pair of boots, and the crooked bills had been picked out and others substituted, it made him feel that starting a republic was a mighty unpopular job.

General Arnold had married a Tory lady, and lived in Philadelphia while recovering from his wounds received at Quebec and Saratoga. He was rather a high roller, and ran behind, so that it is estimated that his bills there per month required a peach-basket-full of currency with which to pay them, as the currency was then quoted. Besides, Gates had worried him, and made him think that patriotism was mostly politics. He was also overbearing, and the people of Philadelphia mobbed him once. He was reprimanded gently by Washington, but Arnold was haughty and yet humiliated. He got command of West Point, a very important place indeed, and then arranged with Clinton to swap it for six thousand three hundred and fifteen pounds and a colonelcy in the English army.

Major André was appointed to confer with Arnold, and got off the ship Vulture to make his way to the appointed place, but it was daylight by that time, and the Vulture, having been fired on, dropped down the river. André now saw no way for him but to get back to New York; but at Tarrytown he was met by three patriots, who caught his horse by the reins, and, though André tried to tip them, he did not succeed. They found papers on his person, among them a copy of *Punch*, which made them suspicious that he was not an American, and so he was tried and hanged as a spy. This was one of the saddest features of the American Revolution, and should teach us to be careful how we go about in an enemy's country, also to use great care in selecting and subscribing for papers.

In 1781, Greene, who succeeded Gates, took charge of the two thousand ragged and bony troops. January 17 he was attacked at Cowpens by Tarleton. The militia fell back, and the English made a grand charge, supposing victory to be within reach. But the wily and foxy troops turned at thirty yards and gave the undertaking business a boom that will never be forgotten.

Morgan was in command of the Colonial forces. He went on looking for more regulars to kill, but soon ran up against Cornwallis the surrenderer.

General Greene now joined Morgan, and took charge of the retreat. At the Yadkin River they crossed over ahead of Cornwallis, when it began for to rain. When Cornwallis came to the river he found it so swollen and restless that he decided not to cross. Later he crossed higher up, and made for the fords of the Dan at thirty miles a day, to head off the Americans. Greene beat him, however, by a length, and saved his troops.

The writer has seen the place on the Yadkin where Cornwallis decided not to cross. It was one of the pivotal points of the war, and is of about medium height.

A fight followed at Guilford Court-House, where the Americans were driven back, but the enemy got thinned out so noticeably that Cornwallis decided to retreat. He went back to Washington on a Bull Run schedule, without pausing even for feed or water. Cornwallis was greatly agitated, and the coat he wore at the time, and now shown in the Smithsonian Institution, shows distinctly the marks made where the Colonists played checkers on the tail.

The battle of Eutaw Springs, September 8, also greatly reduced the British forces at that point.

Arnold conducted a campaign into Virginia, and was very brutal about it, killing a great many people who were strangers to him, and who had never harmed him, not knowing him, as the historian says, from 'Adam's off ox.'

Cornwallis in this Virginia and Southern trip destroyed ten million dollars' worth of property, and then fortified himself at Yorktown.

Washington decided to besiege Yorktown, and, making a feint to fool Clinton, set out for that place, visiting Mount Vernon *en route* after an absence of six and a half years, though only stopping two days. Washington was a soldier in the true sense, and, when a lad, was given a little hatchet by his father. George cut down some cherry-trees with this, in order to get the cherries without climbing the trees. One day his father discovered that the trees had been cut down, and spoke of it to the lad.

'Yes,' said George, 'I did it with my little hatchet; but I would rather cut down a thousand cherry-trees and tell the truth about it than be punished for it.'

'Well said, my brave boy!' exclaimed the happy father as he emptied George's toy bank into his pocket in payment for the trees. 'You took the words right out of my mouth.'

In speaking of the siege of Yorktown, the historian says, 'The most hearty good will prevailed.' What more could you expect of a siege than that?

Cornwallis capitulated October 19. It was the most artistic capitulation he had ever given. The troops were arranged in two lines facing each other, British and American with their allies the French under Rochambeau.

GEORGE'S FATHER TAKING PAY
FOR THE CHERRY-TREES.

People came from all over the country who had heard of Cornwallis and his wonderful genius as a capitulator. They came for miles, and brought their lunches with them; but the general, who felt an unnecessary pique towards Washington, refused to take part in the exercises himself, claiming that by the advice of his physicians he would have to remain in his tent, as they feared that he had over-capitulated himself already. He therefore sent his sword by General O'Hara, and Washington turned it over to Lincoln, who had been obliged to surrender to the English at Charleston.

The news reached Philadelphia in the night, and when the watchman cried, 'Past two o'clock, and Cornwallis is taken!' the people arose and went and prayed and laughed like lunatics, for they regarded the war as virtually ended. The old door-keeper of Congress died of delight. Thanks were returned to Almighty God, and George Washington's nomination was a sure thing.

CORNWALLIS SENDING HIS
SWORD BY GENERAL O'HARA.

England decided that whoever counselled war any further was a
public enemy, and Lord North, then prime minister, when he heard
of the surrender of Cornwallis through a New York paper,
exclaimed, 'Oh, God! it is all over!'

Washington now showed his sagacity in quelling the fears of the
soldiers regarding their back pay. He was invited to become king,
but, having had no practice, and fearing that he might run against a
coup d'état or *faux pas*, he declined, and spoke kindly against taking
violent measures.

In 1783, September 3, a treaty of peace was signed in Paris, and
Washington, delivering the most successful farewell address ever
penned, retired to Mount Vernon, where he began at once to enrich
his farm with the suggestions he had received during his absence,
and to calmly take up the life that had been interrupted by the
tedious and disagreeable war.

The country was free and independent, but, oh, how ignorant it was about the science of government! The author does not wish to be personal when he states that the country at that time did not know enough about affairs to carry water for a circus elephant.

It was heavily in debt, with no power to raise money. New England refused to pay her poll-tax, and a party named Shays directed his hired man to overturn the government; but a felon broke out on his thumb, and before he could put it down the crisis was averted and the country saved.

WASHINGTON BEGAN AT ONCE TO ENRICH HIS FARM.

CHAPTER XIX.

THE FIRST PRESIDENT.

It now became the duty of the new republic to seek out the man to preside over it, and George Washington seems to have had no rivals. He rather reluctantly left his home at Mount Vernon, where he was engaged in trying the rotation of crops, and solemnly took the oath to support the Constitution of the United States, which had been adopted September 17, 1787. His trip in April, 1789, from Mount Vernon to the seat of government in New York was a simple but beautiful ovation.

Everybody tried to make it pleasant for him. He was asked at all the towns to build there, and 'most everybody wanted him 'to come and make their house his home.' When he got to the ferry he was not pushed off into the water by commuters, but lived to reach the Old Federal Hall, where he was sworn in.

In 1791 the seat of government was removed to Philadelphia, where it remained for ten years, after which the United States took advantage of the Homestead Act and located on a tract of land ten miles square, known as the District of Columbia. In 1846 that part of the District lying on the Virginia side of the Potomac was ceded back to the State.

President Washington did not have to escape from the capital to avoid office-seekers. He could get on a horse at his door and in five minutes be out of sight. He could remain in the forest back of his house until Martha blew the horn signifying that the man who wanted the post-office at Pigback had gone, and then he could return.

MARTHA BLEW THE HORN.

How times have changed with the growth of the republic! Now Pigback has grown so that the name has been changed to Hogback, and the President avails himself of every funeral that he can possibly feel an interest in, to leave the swarm of jobless applicants who come to pester him to death for appointments.

The historian begs leave to say here that the usefulness of the President for the good of his country and the consideration of greater questions will some day be reduced to very little unless he may be able to avoid this effort to please voters who overestimate their greatness.

It is said that Washington had no library, which accounted for his originality. He was a vestryman in the Episcopal Church; and to see his tall and graceful form as he moved about from pew to pew collecting pence for Home Missions, was a lovely sight.

As a boy he was well behaved and a careful student.

At one time he was given a hatchet by his father, which — —

But what has the historian to do with this morbid wandering in search of truth?

Things were very much unsettled. England had not sent a minister to this country, and had arranged no commercial treaty with us.

Washington's Cabinet consisted of three portfolios and a rack in which he kept his flute-music.

The three ministers were the Secretary of State, the Secretary of War, and the Secretary of the Treasury. There was no Attorney-General, or Postmaster-General, or Secretary of the Interior, or of the Navy, or Seed Catalogue Secretary.

Hamilton, the Secretary of the Treasury, advised that Congress at the earliest moment provide itself with a national debt, which was done, the war debt being assumed by the Congressional representatives of the thirteen Colonies.

A tax was levied on spirits, and a mint started, combining the two, and making the mint encourage the consumption of spirits, and thus the increase of the tax, very likely.

A Whiskey Rebellion broke out in 1794. Pennsylvania especially rebelled at the tax on this grocery, but it was put down. (Those wishing to know which was put down will find out by consulting the Appendix, which will be issued a year from this winter.)

A few Indian wars now kept the people interested, and a large number of the red brothers, under Little Turtle, soon found themselves in the soup, as Washington put it so tersely in his message the following year. Twenty-five thousand square miles north of the Ohio were obtained by treaty from the Indians.

England claimed that traffic with America was not desirable, as the Americans did not pay their debts. Possibly that was true, for muskrat pelts were low at that time, and England refused to take cord-wood and saw-logs piled on the New York landing as cash.

Chief-Justice Jay was sent to London to confer with the king, which he did. He was not invited, however, to come to the house during his stay, and the queen did not call on Mrs. Jay. The Jays have never recovered from this snub, and are still gently guyed by the comic papers.

But the treaty was negotiated, and now the Americans are said to pay their debts as well as the nobility who marry our American girls instead of going into bankruptcy, as some would do.

The Mississippi and the Mediterranean Sea were opened for navigation to American vessels now, and things looked better, for we could by this means exchange our cranberries for sugar and barter our Indian relics for camel's-hair shawls, of which the pioneers were very much in need during the rigorous winters in the North.

The French now had a difficulty with England, and Washington, who still remembered La Fayette and the generous aid of the French, wished that he was back at Mount Vernon, working out his poll-tax on the Virginia roads, for he was in a tight place.

It was now thought best to have two political parties, in order to enliven editorial thought and expression. So the Republican party, headed by Jefferson, Madison, and Randolph, and the Federalist party, led by Hamilton and Adams, were organized, and public speakers were engaged from a distance.

The latter party supported the administration,—which was not so much of a job as it has been several times since.

Washington declined to accept a third term, and wrote a first-rate farewell address. A lady, whose name is withheld, writing of those times, closes by saying that President Washington was one of the sweetest men she ever knew.

OIL THE GEARING OF THE SOLAR SYSTEM.

John Adams succeeded Washington as President, and did not change his politics to amount to much.

He made a good record as Congressman, but lost it as President largely because of his egotism. He seemed to think that if he neglected to oil the gearing of the solar system about so often, it would stop running. We should learn from this to be humble even when we are in authority. Adams and Jefferson were good friends during the Revolution, but afterwards political differences estranged them till they returned to private life. Adams was a poor judge of men, and offended several members of the press who called on him to get his message in advance.

Our country was on the eve of a war with France, when Napoleon I. was made Consul, and peace followed.

Adams's administration made the Federalists unpopular, owing to the Alien and Sedition laws, and Jefferson was elected the successor of Adams, Burr running as Vice-President with him. The election was so close that it went to the House, however.

Jefferson, or the Sage of Monticello, was a good President, noted for his simplicity. He married and brought his bride home to Monticello prior to this. She had to come on horseback about one hundred miles, and, as the house was unfinished and no servants there, they had to sleep on the work-bench and eat what was left of the carpenter's lunch.

Jeffersonian simplicity was his strong point, and people who called at the White House often found him sprinkling the floor of his office, or trying to start a fire with kerosene.

Burr was Vice-President, and, noticing at once that the office did not attract any attention to speak of, decided to challenge Mr. Alexander Hamilton to fight a duel with him.

The affair took place at Weehawken, July 11, 1804. Hamilton fell at the first fire, on the same spot where his eldest son had been killed in the same way.

Burr went West, and was afterwards accused of treason on the ground that he was trying to organize Mexico against the United States government. He was put in a common jail to await trial. Afterwards he was discharged, but was never again on good terms with the government, and never rose again.

TRYING TO START A FIRE WITH KEROSENE.

The artist has shown us how Burr and Hamilton should have fought, but, alas! they were not progressive men and did not realize this till too late. Another method would have been to use the bloodless method of the French duel, or the newspaper customs adopted by the pugilists of 1893. The time is approaching when mortal combat in America will be confined to belligerent people under the influence of liquor. A newspaper assault instead of a duel might have made Burr President and Hamilton Vice-President.

When he came into town and registered at the hotel the papers did not say anything about it; and so he stopped taking them, thus falling into ignorance and oblivion at the same moment, although at one time he had lacked but a single vote to make him President of the United States.

England and France still continued at war, and American vessels were in hot water a good deal, as they were liable to be overhauled by both parties. England especially, with the excuse that she was looking for deserters, stopped American vessels and searched them, going through the sleeping-apartments before the work was done up,—one of the rudest things known in international affairs.

THE MODERN WAY OF SETTLING DIFFERENCES.

An Embargo Act was passed forbidding American vessels to leave port, an act which showed that the bray of the ass had begun to echo through the halls of legislation even at that early day.

In the mean time, Jefferson had completed his second term, and James Madison, the Republican candidate, had succeeded him at the helm of state, as it was then called.

His party favored a war with England, especially as the British had begun again to stir up the red brother.

NOT TOO HAUGHTY TO HAVE FUN SOMETIMES.

Madison was a Virginian. He was a man of unblemished character, and was not too haughty to have fun sometimes. This endeared him to the whole nation. Unlike Adams, he never swelled up so that his dignity hurt him under the arms. He died in 1836, genial and sunny to the last.

It was now thought best to bring on the war of 1812, which began by an Indian attack at Tippecanoe on General Harrison's troops in 1811, when the Indians were defeated. June 19, 1812, war was finally declared.

The first battle was between the forces under General Hull on our side and the English and Indians on the British side, near Detroit. The troops faced each other, Tecumseh being the Indian leader, and both armies stood ready to have one of the best battles ever given in public or private, when General Hull was suddenly overcome with remorse at the thought of shedding blood, especially among people who were so common, and, shaking a large table-cloth out the window in token of peace, amid the tears of his men, surrendered his entire command in a way that reminded old settlers very much of Cornwallis.

SURRENDER OF GENERAL HULL.

CHAPTER XX.

THE WAR WITH CANADA.

October 13, General Van Rensselaer crossed the Niagara River and attacked the British at Queenstown Heights. The latter retreated, and General Brock was killed. General Van Rensselaer went back after the rest of his troops, but they refused to cross, on the ground that the general had no right to take them out of the United States, and thus the troops left in charge at the Heights were compelled to surrender.

These troops who refused to go over and accept a victory already won for them, because they didn't want to cross the Canadian line, would not have shied so at the boundary if they had been boodlers, very likely, in later years.

August 19 occurred the naval fight between the Constitution and Guerriere, off the Massachusetts coast. The Constitution, called 'Old Ironsides,' was commanded by Captain Isaac Hull. The Guerriere was first to attack, but got no reply until both vessels were very close together, when into her starboard Captain Hull poured such a load of hardware that the Guerriere was soon down by the head and lop-sided on the off side. She surrendered, but was of no value, being so full of holes that she would not hold a cargo of railroad-trestles.

The economy used by the early American warriors by land and sea regarding their ammunition, holding their fire until the enemy was at arm's length, was the cause of more than one victory. They were obliged, indeed, to make every bullet count in the days when even lead was not produced here, and powder was imported.

October 13, the naval fight between the Frolic and Wasp took place, off the North Carolina coast. The Frolic was an English brig, and she wound up as most frolics do, with a severe pain and a five-dollar fine. After the Wasp had called and left her R. S. V. P. cards, the decks of the Frolic were a sight to behold. There were not enough able-bodied men to surrender the ship. She was captured by the boarding-crew, but there was not a man left of her own crew to haul down the colors.

IF THEY HAD BEEN BOODLERS.

Other victories followed on the sea, and American privateers had more fun than anybody.

Madison was re-elected, thus showing that his style of administration suited one and all, and the war was prosecuted at a great rate. It became a sort of fight with Canada, the latter being supported by English arms by land and sea. Of course the Americans would have preferred to fight England direct, and many were in favor of attacking London: but when the commanding officer asked those of the army who had the means to go abroad to please raise their right hands, it was found that the trip must be abandoned. Those who had the means to go did not have suitable clothes for making a respectable appearance, and so it was given up.

Three divisions were made of the army, all having an attack on Canada as the object in view,—viz., the army of the Centre, the army of the North, and the army of the West. The armies of the Centre and North did not do much, aside from the trifling victory at York, and President Madison said afterwards in a letter to the writer's family that the two armies did not accomplish enough to pay the duty on them. The army of the West managed to stand off the British, though the latter still held Michigan and threatened Ohio.

BUILDING THE FLEET, MEANTIME BOARDING HIMSELF.

September 10, Perry's victory on Lake Erie occurred, and was well received. Perry was twenty-seven years old, and was given command of a flotilla on Lake Erie, provided he would cut the timber and build it, meantime boarding himself. The British had long been in possession of Lake Erie, and when Perry got his scows afloat they issued invitations for a general display of carnage. They bore down on Perry and killed all the men on his flag-ship but eight. Then he helped them fire the last gun, and with the flag they jumped into a boat which they paddled for the Niagara under a galling fire. This was the first time that a galling fire had ever been used at sea. Perry passed within pistol-shot of the British, and in less than a quarter of an hour after he trod the poop of the Niagara he was able to write to General Harrison, 'We have met the enemy, and they are ours.'

Proctor and Tecumseh were at Malden, with English and Indians, preparing to plunder the frontier and kill some more women and children as soon as they felt rested up. At the news of Perry's victory, Harrison decided to go over and stir them up. Arriving at Malden, he found it deserted, and followed the foe to the river Thames, where he charged with his Kentucky horsemen right through the British lines and so on down the valley, where they reformed and started back to charge on their rear, when the whole outfit surrendered except the Indians. Proctor, however, was mounted on a tall fox-hunter which ran away with him. He afterwards wrote back to General Harrison that he made every effort to surrender personally, but that circumstances prevented. He was greatly pained by this.

The Americans now charged on the Indians, and Johnson, the commander of the Blue Grass Dragoons, fired a shot which took Tecumseh just west of the watch-pocket. He died, he said, tickled to death to know that he had been shot by an American.

PROCTOR ON A TALL FOX-HUNTER WHICH RAN AWAY WITH HIM.

Captain Lawrence, of the Hornet, having taken the British brig Peacock, was given command of the Chesapeake, which he took to Boston to have repaired. While there, he got a challenge from the Shannon. He put to sea with half a crew, and a shot in his chest— that is, the arm-chest of the ship—burst the whole thing open and annoyed every one on board. The enemy boarded the Chesapeake and captured her, so Captain Lawrence, her brave commander, breathed his last, after begging his men not to give up the ship.

However, the victories on the Canadian border settled the war once more for the time, and cheered the Americans very much.

The Indians in 1813 fell upon Fort Mimms and massacred the entire garrison, men, women, and children, not because they felt a personal antipathy towards them, but because they—the red brothers—had sold their lands too low and their hearts were sad in their bosoms. There is really no fun in trading with an Indian, for he is devoid of business instincts, and reciprocity with the red brother has never been a success.

General Jackson took some troops and attacked the red brother, killing six hundred of him and capturing the rest of the herd. Jackson did not want to hear the Indians speak pieces and see them smoke the pipe of peace, but buried the dead and went home. He had very little of the romantic complaint which now and then breaks out regarding the Indian, but knew full well that all the Indians ever born on the face of the earth could not compensate for the cruel and violent death of one good, gentle, patient American mother.

Admiral Cockburn now began to pillage the coast of the Southern States and borrow communion services from the churches of Virginia and the Carolinas. He also murdered the sick in their beds.

Perhaps a word of apology is due the Indians after all. Possibly they got their ideas from Cockburn.

The battle of Lundy's Lane had been arranged for July 25, 1814, and so the Americans crossed Niagara under General Brown to invade Canada. General Winfield Scott led the advance, and gained a brilliant victory, July 5, at Chippewa. The second engagement was at Lundy's Lane, within the sound of the mighty cataract. Old man Lundy, whose lane was used for the purpose, said that it was one of the bloodiest fights, by a good many gallons, that he ever attended. The battle was, however, barren of results, the historian says, though really an American victory from the stand-point of the tactician and professional gore-spiller.

In September, Sir George Prevost took twelve thousand veteran troops who had served under Wellington, and started for Plattsburg.

The ships of the British at the same time opened fire on the nine-dollar American navy, and were almost annihilated. The troops under Prevost started in to fight, but, learning of the destruction of the British fleet on Lake Champlain, Prevost fled like a frightened fawn, leaving his sick and wounded and large stores of lime-juice, porridge, and plum-pudding. The Americans, who had been living on chopped horse-feed and ginseng-root, took a week off and gave themselves up to the false joys of lime-juice and general good feeling.

HIS RAINBOW SMILE.

Along the coast the British destroyed everything they could lay their hands on; but perhaps the rudest thing they did was to enter Washington and burn the Capitol, the Congressional library, and the smoke-house in which President Madison kept his hams. Even now, when the writer is a guest of some great English dignitary, and perhaps at table picking the 'merry-thought' of a canvas-back duck, the memory of this thing comes over him, and, burying his face in the costly napery, he gives himself up to grief until kind words and a celery-glass-full of turpentine, or something, bring back his buoyancy and rainbow smile. The hospitality and generous treatment of our English brother to Americans now is something beautiful, unaffected, and well worth a voyage across the qualmy sea to see, but when Cockburn burned down the Capitol and took the President's sugar-cured hams he did a rude act.

CHAPTER XXI.

THE ADVANCE OF THE REPUBLIC.

The administration now began to suffer at the hands of the people, many of whom criticised the conduct of the war and that of the President also. People met at Hartford and spoke so harshly that the Hartford Federalist obtained a reputation which clung to him for many years.

There being no cable in those days, the peace by Treaty of Ghent was not heard of in time to prevent the battle of New Orleans, January 8, 1815, there having been two weeks of peace as a matter of fact when this hot and fatal battle was fought.

General Pakenham, with a force of twelve thousand men by sea and land, attacked the city. The land forces found General Jackson intrenched several miles below the city. He had used cotton for fortifications at first, but a hot shot had set a big bunch of it on fire and rolled it over towards the powder-supplies, so that he did not use cotton any more.

General Pakenham was met by the solid phalanx of Tennessee and Kentucky riflemen, who reserved their fire, as usual, until the loud uniform of the English could be distinctly heard, when they poured into their ranks a galling fire, as it was so tersely designated at the time. General Pakenham fell mortally wounded, and his troops were repulsed, but again rallied, only to be again repulsed. This went on until night, when General Lambert, who succeeded General Pakenham, withdrew, hopelessly beaten, and with a loss of over two thousand men.

The United States now found that an honorable peace had been obtained, and with a debt of $127,000,000 started in to pay it up by instalments, which was done inside of twenty years from the ordinary revenue.

In the six years following, one State per year was added to the Union, and all kinds of manufactures were built up to supply the goods that had been cut off by the blockade during the war. Even the deluge of cheap goods from abroad after the war did not succeed in breaking these down.

James Monroe was almost unanimously elected. He was generally beloved, and his administration was, in fact, known as the original 'era of good feeling,' since so successfully reproduced especially by the Governors of North and South Carolina. (See Appendix.)

Through the efforts of Henry Clay, Missouri was admitted as a slave State in 1821, under the compromise that slavery should not be admitted into any of the Territories west of the Mississippi and north of parallel 36° 30' N.

Clay was one of the greatest men of his time, and was especially eminent as an eloquent and magnetic speaker in the days when the record for eloquence was disputed by the giants of American oratory, and before the Senate of the United States had become a wealthy club of men whose speeches are rarely printed except at so much per column, paid in advance.

Clay was the original patentee of the slogan for campaign use.

Lafayette revisited this country in 1819, and was greeted with the greatest hospitality. He visited the grave of Washington, and tenderly spoke of the grandeur of character shown by his chief.

He was given the use of the Brandywine, a government ship, for his return. As he stood on the deck of the vessel at Pier 1, North River, his mind again recurred to Washington, and to those on shore he said that 'to show Washington's love of truth, even as a child, he could tell an interesting incident of him relating to a little new hatchet given him at the time by his father.' As he reached this point in his remarks, Lafayette noted with surprise that some one had slipped his cable from shore and his ship was gently shoved off by people on the pier, while his voice was drowned in the notes of the New York Oompah Oompah Band as it struck up 'Johnny, git yer Gun.'

Florida was ceded to the United States in the same year by Spain, and was sprinkled over with a light coating of sand for the waves to monkey with. The Everglades of Florida are not yet under cultivation.

Mr. Monroe became the author of what is now called the 'Monroe doctrine,' — viz., that the effort of any foreign country to obtain dominion in America would thereafter and forever afterwards be regarded as an unfriendly act. Rather than be regarded as unfriendly, foreign countries now refrain from doing their dominion or dynasty work here.

The Whigs now appeared, and the old Republican party became known as the Democratic party. John Quincy Adams and Henry Clay were Whigs, and John C. Calhoun and Andrew Jackson were Democrats. The Whigs favored a high protective tariff and internal improvement. The Democrats did not favor anything especially, but bitterly opposed the Whig measures, whatever they were.

BALD-HEADED MEN NOT APPRECIATED.

In 1825, John Quincy Adams, son of John Adams, was elected President, and served one term. He was a bald-headed man, and the country was given four years of unexampled prosperity. Yet this experience has not been regarded by the people as it should have been. Other kinds of men have repeatedly been elected to that office, only to bring sorrow, war, debt, and bank-failures upon us. Sometimes it would seem to the thinking mind that, as a people, we need a few car-loads of sense in each school-district, where it can be used at a moment's notice.

Adams was not re-elected, on account of his tariff ideas, which were not popular at the South. He was called 'The old man eloquent,' and it is said that during his more impassioned passages his head, which was round and extremely smooth, became flushed, so that, from resembling the cue-ball on the start, as he rose to more lofty heights his dome of thought looked more like the spot ball on a billiard-table. No one else in Congress at that time had succeeded in doing this.

John Quincy Adams was succeeded in 1829 by Andrew Jackson, the hero of New Orleans. Jackson was the first to introduce what he called 'rotation in office.' During the forty years previous there had been but seventy-four removals; Jackson made seven hundred. This custom has been pretty generally adopted since, giving immense satisfaction to those who thrive upon the excitement of offensive partisanship and their wives' relations, while those who have legitimate employment and pay taxes support and educate a new official kindergarten with every change of administration.

The prophet sees in the distance an eight-year term for the President, and employment thereafter as 'charge-d'affaires' of the United States, with permission to go beyond the seas. Thus the vast sums of money and rivers of rum used in the intervening campaigns at present will be used for the relief of the widow and orphan. The ex-President then, with the portfolio of International Press Agent for the United States, could go abroad and be fêted by foreign governments, leaving dyspepsia everywhere in his wake and crowned heads with large damp towels on them.

Every ex-President should have some place where he could go and hide his shame. A trip around the world would require a year, and by that time the voters would be so disgusted with the new President that the old one would come like a healing balm, and he would be permitted to die without publishing a bulletin of his temperature and showing his tongue to the press for each edition of the paper.

South Carolina in 1832 passed a nullification act declaring the tariff act 'null and void' and announcing that the State would secede from the Union if force were used to collect any revenue at Charleston. South Carolina has always been rather 'advanced' regarding the matter of seceding from the American Union.

President Jackson, however, ordered General Scott and a number of troops to go and see that the laws were enforced; but no trouble resulted, and soon more satisfactory measures were enacted, through the large influence of Mr. Clay.

Jackson was unfriendly to the Bank of the United States, and the bank retaliated by contracting its loans, thus making money-matters hard to get hold of by the masses.

'When the public money,' says the historian, 'which had been withdrawn from the Bank of the United States was deposited in local banks, money was easy and speculation extended to every branch of trade. New cities were laid out; fabulous prices were charged for building-lots which existed only on paper' etc. And in Van Buren's time the people paid the violinist, as they have in 1893, with ruin and remorse.

Speculation which is unprofitable should never be encouraged. Unprofitable speculation is only another term for idiocy. But, on the other hand, profitable speculation leads to prosperity, public esteem, and the ability to keep a team. We may distinguish the one from the other by means of ascertaining the difference between them. If one finds on waking up in the morning that he experiences a sensation of being in the poor-house, he may almost at once jump to the conclusion that the kind of speculation he selected was the wrong one.

SCALPING A MAN BETWEEN THE SOUP
AND THE REMOVE.

The Black Hawk War occurred in the Northwest Territory in 1832. It grew out of the fact that the Sacs and Foxes sold their lands to the United States and afterwards regretted that they had not asked more for them: so they refused to vacate, until several of them had been used up on the asparagus-beds of the husbandman.

The Florida War (1835) grew out of the fact that the Seminoles regretted having made a dicker with the government at too low a price for land. Osceola, the chief, regretted the matter so much that he scalped General Thompson while the latter was at dinner, which shows that the Indian is not susceptible to cultivation or the acquisition of any knowledge of table etiquette whatever. What could be in poorer taste than scalping a man between the soup and the remove? The same day Major Dade with one hundred men was waylaid, and all but four of the party killed.

Seven years later the Indians were subdued.

Phrenologically the Indian allows his alimentiveness to overbalance his group of organs which show veneration, benevolence, fondness for society, fêtes champêtres, etc., hope, love of study, fondness for agriculture, an unbridled passion for toil, etc.

France owed five million dollars for damages to our commerce in Napoleon's wars, and, Napoleon himself being entirely worthless, having said every time that the bill was presented that he would settle it as soon as he got back from St. Helena, Jackson ordered reprisals to be made, but England acted as a peacemaker, and the bill was paid. On receiving the money a trunk attached by our government and belonging to Napoleon was released.

Space here, and the nature of this work, forbid an extended opinion regarding the course pursued by Napoleon in this matter. His tomb is in the basement of the Hôtel des Invalides in Paris, and you are requested not to *fumer* while you are there.

FITTED IN PARIS AT GREAT EXPENSE.

CHAPTER XXII.

MORE DIFFICULTIES STRAIGHTENED OUT.

Van Buren, the eighth President, was unfortunate in taking the helm as the financial cyclone struck the country. This was brought about by scarcity of funds more than anything else. Business-men would not pay their debts, and, though New York was not then so large as at present, one hundred million dollars were lost in sixty days in this way.

The government had required the payments for public lands to be made in coin, and so the Treasury had plenty of gold and silver, while business had nothing to work with. Speculation also had made a good many snobs who had sent their gold and silver abroad for foreign luxuries, also some paupers who could not do so. When a man made some money from the sale of rural lots he had his hats made abroad, and his wife had her dresses fitted in Paris at great expense. Confidence was destroyed, and the air was heavy with failures and apprehension of more failures to come.

The Canadians rebelled against England, and many of our people wanted to unite with Canada against the mother-country, but the police would not permit them to do so. General Scott was sent to the frontier to keep our people from aiding the Canadians.

There was trouble in the Northeast over the boundary between Maine and New Brunswick, but it was settled by the commissioners, Daniel Webster and Lord Ashburton. Webster was a smart man and a good extemporaneous speaker.

LORD ASHBURTON AND DANIEL WEBSTER.

Van Buren failed of a re-election, as the people did not fully endorse his administration. Administrations are not generally endorsed where the people are unable to get over six pounds of sugar for a dollar.

General Harrison, who followed in 1841, died soon after choosing his Cabinet, and his Vice-President, John Tyler, elected as a Whig, proceeded to act as President, but not as a Whig President should. His party passed a bill establishing the United States Bank, but Tyler vetoed it, and the men who elected him wished they had been as dead as Rameses was at the time.

Dorr's justly celebrated rebellion in Rhode Island was an outbreak resulting from restricting the right of suffrage to those who owned property. A new Constitution was adopted, and Dorr chosen as Governor. He was not recognized, and so tried to capture the seat while the regular governor was at tea. He got into jail for life, but was afterwards pardoned out and embraced the Christian religion.

In 1844 the Anti-Rent War in the State of New York broke out among those who were tenants of the old 'Patroon Estates.' These men, disguised as Indians, tarred and feathered those who paid rent, and killed the collectors who were sent to them. In 1846 the matter was settled by the military.

TARRED AND FEATHERED FOR PAYING RENT.

In 1840 the Mormons had settled at Nauvoo, Illinois. They were led by Joseph Smith, and not only proposed to run a new kind of religion, but introduced polygamy into it. The people who lived near them attacked them, killed Smith, and drove the Mormons to Iowa, opposite Omaha.

In 1844 occurred the building of the magnetic telegraph, invented by Samuel F. B. Morse. The line was from Baltimore to Washington, or *vice versa*,—authorities failing to agree on this matter. It cost thirty thousand dollars, and the boys who delivered the messages made more out of it then than the stockholders did.

THE MESSENGER-BOYS MADE MORE OUT
OF IT THAN THE STOCKHOLDERS.

Fulton having invented and perfected the steamboat in 1805 and started the Clermont on the North River at the dizzy rate of five miles per hour, and George Stephenson having in 1814 made the first locomotive to run on a track, the people began to feel that theosophy was about all they needed to place them on a level with the seraphim and other astral bodies.

Texas had, under the guidance of Sam Houston, obtained her independence from Mexico, and asked for admission to the Union. Congress at first rejected her, fearing that the Texas people lacked cultivation, being so far away from the thought-ganglia of the East,

169

also fearing a war with Mexico; but she was at last admitted, and now every one is glad of it.

The Whigs were not in favor of the admission of Texas, and made that the issue of the following campaign, Henry Clay leading his party to a hospitable grave in the fall. James K. Polk, a Democrat, was elected. His rallying cry was, 'I am a Democrat.'

The Mexican War now came on. General Taylor's army met the enemy first at Palo Alto, where he ran across the Mexicans six thousand strong, and, though he had but two thousand men, drove them back, only losing nine men. This was the most economical battle of the war.

The next afternoon he met the enemy at Resaca de la Palma, and whipped him in the time usually required to ejaculate the word 'scat!'

Next General Taylor proceeded against Monterey, September 24, and with six thousand men attacked the strongly-fortified city, which held ten thousand troops. The Americans avoided the heavy fire as well as possible by entering the city and securing rooms at the best hotel, leaving word at the office that they did not wish to be disturbed by the enemy. In fact, the soldiers did dig their way through from house to house to avoid the volleys from the windows, and thus fought to within a square of the Grand Plaza, when the city surrendered. The Grand Plaza is generally a sandy vacant lot, where Mexicans sell *tamales* made of the highly-peppered but tempting cutlets of the Mexican hairless dog.

The battle of Buena Vista took place February 23, 1847, General Santa Anna commanding the Mexicans. He had twenty thousand men, and General Taylor's troops were reduced in numbers. The fight was a hot one, lasting all day, and the Americans were saved by Bragg's artillery. Bragg used the old Colonial method of rolling his guns up to the nose of the enemy and then discharging an iron-foundry into his midst. This disgusted the enemy so that General Santa Anna that evening took the shreds of his army and went away.

THE FIGHT WAS A HOT ONE.

General Kearney was sent to take New Mexico and California. His work consisted mainly in marching for General Frémont, who had been surveying a new route to Oregon, and had with sixty men been so successful that on the arrival of Kearney, with the aid of Commodores Sloat and Stockton, California was captured, and has given general satisfaction to every one.

In March, 1847, General Scott, with twelve thousand men, bombarded Vera Cruz four days, and at the end of that time the city was surrendered.

At Cerro Gordo, a week later, Scott overtook the enemy under General Santa Anna, and made such a fierce attack that the Mexicans were completely routed. Santa Anna left his leg on the field of battle and rode away on a pet mule named Charlotte Corday. The leg was preserved and taken to the Smithsonian Institute. It is made of second-growth hickory, and has a brass ferrule and a rubber eraser on the end. General Taylor afterwards taunted him with this incident, and, though greatly irritated, Santa Anna said there was no use trying to kick.

Puebla resisted not, and the army marched into the city of Mexico August 7. The road was rendered disagreeable by strong fortifications and thirty thousand men who were not on good terms with Scott. The environments and suburbs one after another were taken, and a parley for peace ensued, during which the Mexicans were busy fortifying some more on the quiet.

September 8 the Americans made their assault, and carried the outworks one by one. Then the castle of Chapultepec was stormed. First the outer works were scaled, which made them much more desirable, and the moat was removed by means of a stomach-pump and blotting-pad, and then the escarpment was up-ended, the Don John tower was knocked silly by a solid shot, and the castle capitulated.

Thus on the 14th of September the old flag floated over the court-house of Mexico, and General Scott ate his tea in the palace of the Montezumas. Peace was declared February 2, 1848, and the United States owned the vast country southward to the Gila (pronounced Heeler) and west to the Pacific Ocean.

The Wilmot Proviso was invented by David Wilmot, a poor, struggling member of Congress, who moved that in any territory acquired by the United States slavery should be prohibited except upon the advice of a physician. The motion was lost.

Gold was discovered in the Sacramento Valley in August, 1848, by a workman who was building a mill-race. A struggle ensued over this ground as to who should own the race. It threatened to terminate in a race war, but was settled amicably.

In eighteen months one hundred thousand people went to the scene. Thousands left their skeletons with the red brother, and other thousands left theirs on the Isthmus of Panama or on the cruel desert. Many married men went who had been looking a long time for some good place to go to. Leaving their wives with ill-concealed relief, they started away through a country filled with death, to reach a country they knew not of. Some died *en route*, others were hanged, and still others became the heads of new families. Some came back and carried water for their wives to wash clothing for their neighbors.

SOME CAME BACK AND CARRIED WATER FOR THEIR WIVES
TO WASH CLOTHING.

It was a long hard trip then across the plains. One of the author's friends at the age of thirteen years drove a little band of cows from the State of Indiana to Sacramento. He says he would not do it again for anything. He is now a man, and owns a large prune-orchard in California, and people tell him he is getting too stout, and that he ought to exercise more, and that he ought to walk every day several miles; but he shakes his head, and says, 'No, I will not walk any to-day, and possibly not to-morrow or the day following. Do not come to me and refer to taking a walk: I have tried that. Possibly you take me for a dromedary; but you are wrong. I am a fat man, and may die suddenly some day while lacing up my shoes, but when I go anywhere I ride.'

When he got to Sacramento, where gold was said to be so plentiful, he was glad to wash dishes for his board, and he went and hired himself out to a citizen of that country, and he sent him into the fields for to feed swine, and he would fain have filled his system with the California peaches which the swine did eat, and he began to be in want, and no man gave unto him, and if he had spent his substance in riotous living, he said, it would have been different.

About thirty years after that he arose and went unto his father, and carried his dinner with him, also a government bond and a new suit of raiment for the old gentleman.

I do not know what we should learn from this.

CHAPTER XXIII.

THE WEBSTERS.

Daniel Webster, together with Mr. Clay, had much to do with the Compromise measures of 1850. These consisted in the admission of California as a free State, the organizing of the Territories of Utah and New Mexico without any provision regarding slavery pro or con, the payment to Texas of one hundred million dollars for New Mexico,—which was a good trade for Texas,—the prohibition of the slave-trade in the District of Columbia, and the enactment of a Fugitive Slave Law permitting owners of slaves to follow them into the free States and take them back in irons, if necessary. The officials and farmers of the free States were also expected to turn out, call the dog, leave their work, and help catch these chattels and carry them to the south-bound train.

Daniel Webster was born in 1782, and Noah in 1758. Daniel was educated at Dartmouth College, where he was admitted in 1797. He taught school winters and studied summers, as many other great men have done since, until he knew about everything that anybody could. What Dan did not know, Noah did.

Strange to say, Daniel was frightened to death when first called upon to speak a piece. He says he committed dozens of pieces to memory and recited them to the woods and crags and cows and stone abutments of the New England farms, but could not stand up before a school and utter a word.

In 1801 he studied law with Thomas W. Thompson, afterwards United States Senator. He read then for the first time that 'Law is a rule of action prescribing what is right and prohibiting what is wrong.'

In 1812 he was elected to Congress, and in 1813 made his maiden speech. One of his most masterly speeches was made on economical and financial subjects; and yet in order to get his blue broadcloth

coat with brass buttons from the tailor-shop to wear while making
the speech, he had to borrow twenty-five dollars.

DANIEL WEBSTER COULD NOT STAND UP BEFORE A SCHOOL
AND UTTER A WORD.

When the country has wanted a man to talk well on these subjects it
has generally been compelled to advance money to him before he
could make a speech. Sometimes he has to be taken from the pawn-
shop. Webster, it is said, was the most successful lawyer, after he
returned to Boston, that the State of Massachusetts has ever known;
and yet his mail was full of notices from banks down East,
announcing that he had overdrawn his account.

Once he was hard pressed for means, as he was trying to run a farm,
and running a farm costs money: so he went to a bank to borrow. He
hated to do it, because he had no special inducements to offer a bank
or to make it hilariously loan him money.

'How much did you think you would need, Mr. Webster?' asked the
President, cutting off some coupons as he spoke and making paper
dolls of them.

'Well, I could get along very well,' said Webster, in that deep, resinous voice of his, 'if I could have two thousand dollars.'

'Well, you remember,' said the banker, 'do you not, that you have two thousand dollars here, that you deposited five years ago, after you had dined with the Governor of North Carolina?'

'No, I had forgotten about that,' said Webster. 'Give me a blank check without unnecessary delay.'

We may learn from this that Mr. Webster was not a careful man in the matter of detail.

His speech on the two-hundredth anniversary of the landing of the Pilgrims was a good thing, and found its way into the press of the time. His speech at the laying of the corner-stone of the Bunker Hill Monument, and his eulogy of Adams and Jefferson, were beautiful and thrilling.

Daniel Webster had a very large brain, and used to loan his hat to brother Senators now and then when their heads were paining them, provided he did not want it himself.

His reply to Robert Y. Hayne, of South Carolina, in 1830, was regarded as one of his ablest parliamentary efforts. Hayne attacked New England, and first advanced the doctrine of nullification, which was even more dangerous than secession, — Jefferson Davis in 1860 denying that he had ever advocated or favored such a doctrine.

Webster spoke extempore, and people sent out for their lunch rather than go away in the midst of his remarks.

Webster married twice, but did not let that make any difference with his duty to his country.

He tried to farm it some, but did not amass a large sum, owing to his heavy losses in trying year after year to grow Saratoga potatoes for the Boston market.

No American, foreign or domestic, ever made a greater name for himself than Daniel Webster, but he was not so good a penman as Noah; Noah was the better pen-writer.

SENT OUT FOR THEIR LUNCH RATHER THAN GO AWAY IN
THE MIDST OF HIS REMARKS.

Noah Webster also had the better command of language of the two.
Those who have read his great work entitled 'Webster's Elementary
Spelling-Book, or, How One Word Led to Another,' will agree with
me that he was smart. Noah never lacked for a word by which to
express himself. He was a brainy man and a good speller.

One by one our eminent men are passing away. Mr. Webster has
passed away; Napoleon Bonaparte is no more; and Dr. Mary Walker

is fading away. This has been a severe winter on Red Shirt; and I have to guard against the night air a good deal myself.

It would ill become me, at this late date, to criticise Mr. Webster's work, a work that is now, I may say, in nearly every home and school-room in the land. It is a great book. I only hope that had Mr. Webster lived he would have been equally fair in his criticism of my books.

I hate to compare my books with Mr. Webster's, because it looks egotistical in me; but, although Noah's book is larger than mine, and has more literary attractions as a book to set a child on at the table, it does not hold the interest of the reader all the way through.

He has introduced too many characters into his book at the expense of the plot. It is a good book to pick up and while away a leisure hour, perhaps, but it is not a work that could rivet your interest till midnight, while the fire went out and the thermometer stepped down to 47° below zero. You do not hurry through the pages to see whether Reginald married the girl or not. Mr. Webster did not seem to care how the affair turned out.

NEVER LEFT HIS ROOM TILL HE HAD DEVOURED IT.

Therein consists the great difference between Noah and myself. He doesn't keep up the interest. A friend of mine at Sing Sing, who secured one of my books, said he never left his room till he had devoured it. He said he seemed chained to the spot; and if you can't believe a convict who is entirely out of politics, whom, in the name of George Washington, can you trust?

Mr. Webster was certainly a most brilliant writer, though a little inclined, perhaps, to be wordy. I have discovered in some of his later books one hundred and eighteen thousand words no two of which are alike. This shows great fluency and versatility, it is true, but we need something else. The reader waits in vain to be thrilled by the author's wonderful word-painting. There is not a thrill in the whole tome.

I had heard so much of Mr. Webster that when I read his book I confess I was disappointed. It is cold, methodical, dry, and dispassionate in the extreme, and one cannot help comparing it with the works of James Fenimore Cooper and Horace.

As I said, however, it is a good book to pick up for the purpose of whiling away an idle hour. No one should travel without Mr. Webster's tale. Those who examine this tale will readily see why there were no flies on the author. He kept them off with this tale.

It is a good book, as I say, to take up for a moment, or to read on the train, or to hold the door open on a hot day. I would never take a long railroad ride without it, eyether. I would as soon forget my bottle of cough-medicine.

Mr. Webster's Speller had an immense sale. Ten years ago he had sold forty million copies. And yet it had this same defect. It was cold, dull, disconnected, and verbose. There was only one good thing in the book, and that was a little literary gem regarding a boy who broke in and stole the apples of a total stranger. The story was so good that I have often wondered whom Mr. Webster got to write it for him.

The old man, it seems, at first told the boy that he had better come down, as there was a draught in the tree; but the young sass-box—apple-sass-box, I presume—told him to avaunt.

At last the old man said, 'Come down, honey. I am afraid the limb will break if you don't.' Then, as the boy still remained, he told him that those were not eating-apples, that they were just common cooking-apples, and that there were worms in them. But the boy said he didn't mind a little thing like that. So then the old gentleman got irritated, and called the dog, and threw turf at the boy, and at last saluted him with pieces of turf and decayed cabbages; and after the lad had gone away the old man pried the bull-dog's jaws open and found a mouthful of pantaloons and a freckle.

I do not tell this, of course, in Mr. Webster's language, but I give the main points as they recur now to my mind.

Though I have been a close student of Mr. Webster for years and have carefully examined his style, I am free to say that his ideas about writing a book are not the same as mine. Of course it is a great temptation for a young author to write a book that will have a large sale; but that should not be all. We should have a higher object than that, and strive to interest those who read the book. It should not be jerky and scattering in its statements.

I do not wish to do an injustice to a great man who is now no more, a man who did so much for the world and who could spell the longest word without hesitation, but I speak of these things just as I would expect others to criticise my work. If one aspire to be a member of the *literati* of his day, he must expect to be criticised. I have been criticised myself. When I was in public life,—as a justice of the peace in the Rocky Mountains,—a man came in one day and criticised me so that I did not get over it for two weeks.

I might add, though I dislike to speak of it now, that Mr. Webster was at one time a member of the Legislature of Massachusetts. I believe that was the only time he ever stepped aside from the strait and narrow way. A good many people do not know this, but it is true.

Mr. Webster was also a married man, yet he never murmured or repined.

CHAPTER XXIV.

BEFO' THE WAH—CAUSES WHICH LED TO IT—MASTERLY
GRASP OF THE SUBJECT SHOWN BY THE AUTHOR.

A Man named Lopez in 1851 attempted to annex Cuba, thus
furnishing for our Republican wrapper a genuine Havana filler;
but he failed, and was executed, while his plans were not.

Franklin Pierce was elected President on the Democratic ticket,
running against General Scott, the Whig candidate. Slavery began
to be discussed again, when Stephen A. Douglas, in Congress,
advocated squatter sovereignty, or the right for each Territory to
decide whether it would be a free or a slave State. The measure
became a law in 1854.

That was what made trouble in Kansas. The two elements, free
and slave, were arrayed against each other, and for several years
friends from other States had to come over and help Kansas bury
its dead. The condition of things for some time was exceedingly
mortifying to the citizen who went out to milk after dark without
his gun.

Trouble with Mexico arose, owing to the fact that the government
had used a poor and unreliable map in establishing the line: so
General Gadsden made a settlement for the disputed ground, and
we paid Mexico ten millions of dollars. It is needless to say that
we have since seen the day when we wished that we had it back.

Two ports of entry were now opened to us in Japan by
Commodore Perry's Expedition, and cups and saucers began to
be more plentiful in this country, many of the wealthier deciding
at that time not to cool tea in the saucer or drink it vociferously
from that vessel. This custom and the Whig party passed away at
the same time.

EXCEEDINGLY MORTIFYING TO THE CITIZEN WHO WENT TO
MILK WITHOUT HIS GUN.

The Republican or Anti-Slavery party nominated for President John
C. Frémont, who received the vote of eleven States, but James
Buchanan was elected, and proved to the satisfaction of the world
that there is nothing to prevent any unemployed man's applying for
the Presidency of the United States; also that if his life has been free
from ideas and opinions he may be elected sometimes where one
who has been caught in the very act of thinking, and had it proved
on him, might be defeated.

Chief Justice Taney now stated that slaves could be taken into any
State of the Union by their owners without forfeiting the rights of
ownership. This was called the Dred Scott decision, and did much to
irritate Abolitionists like John Brown, whose soul as this book goes
to press is said to be marching on. Brown was a Kansas man with a
mission and massive whiskers. He would be called now a crank; but
his action in seizing a United States arsenal at Harper's Ferry and
declaring the slaves free was regarded by the South as thoroughly
representative of the Northern feeling.

The country now began to be in a state of restlessness. Brown had
been captured and hanged as a traitor. Northern men were obliged
to leave their work every little while to catch a negro, crate him, and

return him to his master or give him a lift towards Canada; and, as the negro was replenishing the earth at an astonishing rate, general alarm broke out.

OBLIGED TO LEAVE THEIR WORK EVERY LITTLE WHILE TO CATCH A NEGRO.

Douglas was the champion of squatter sovereignty, John C. Breckinridge of the doctrine that slaves could be checked through as personal baggage into any State of the Union, and Lincoln of the anti-slavery principle which afterwards constituted the spinal column of the Federal Government as opposed to the Confederacy of the seceded States.

Lincoln was elected, which reminded him of an anecdote. Douglas and several other candidates were defeated, which did not remind them of anything.

South Carolina seceded in December, 1860, and soon after Mississippi, Florida, Alabama, Georgia, Louisiana, and Texas followed suit.

The following February the Confederacy was organized at Montgomery, Alabama, and Jefferson Davis was elected President. Long and patient effort on the part of the historian to ascertain how he liked it has been entirely barren of results. Alexander H. Stephens was made Vice-President.

Everything belonging to the United States and not thoroughly fastened down was carried away by the Confederacy, while President Buchanan looked the other way or wrote airy persiflage to tottering dynasties which slyly among themselves characterized him as a neat and cleanly old lady.

Had Buchanan been a married man it is generally believed now that his wife would have prevented the war. Then she would have called James out from under the bed and allowed him to come to the table for his meals with the family. But he was not married, and the war came on.

Major Anderson was afraid to remain at Fort Moultrie in Charleston Harbor, so crossed over to Fort Sumter. The South regarded this as hostility, and the fort was watched to see if any one should attempt to divide his lunch with the garrison, which it was declared would be regarded as an act of defiance. The reader will see by this that a deaf and dumb asylum in Northern Michigan was about the only safe place for a peaceable man at that time.

President Lincoln found himself placed at the head of a looted government on the sharp edge of a crisis that had not been properly upholstered. The Buchanan cabinet had left little except a burglar's tool or two here and there to mark its operations, and, with the aged and infirm General Scott at the head of a little army, and no encouragement except from the Abolitionists, many of whom had never seen a colored man outside of a minstrel performance, the President stole incog. into Washington, like a man who had agreed to lecture there.

Southern officers resigned daily from the army and navy to go home and join the fortunes of their several States. Meantime, the Federal government moved about like a baby elephant loaded with shot, while the new Confederacy got men, money, arms, and munitions of war from every conceivable point.

Finding that supplies were to be sent to Major Anderson, General Peter G. T. Beauregard summoned Major Anderson to surrender. General Beauregard, after the war, became one of the good, kind gentlemen who annually stated over their signatures that they had examined the Louisiana State Lottery and that there was no deception about it. The Lottery felt grateful for this, and said that the general should never want while it had a roof of its own.

Major Anderson had seventy men, while General Beauregard had seven thousand. After a bombardment and a general fight of thirty-four hours, the starved and suffocated garrison yielded to overwhelming numbers.

President Lincoln was not admired by a class of people in the North and South who heard with horror that he had at one time worked for ten dollars a month. They thought the President's salary too much for him, and feared that he would buy watermelons with it. They also feared that some day he might tell a funny story in the presence of Queen Victoria. The snobocracy could hardly sleep nights for fear that Lincoln at a state dinner might put sugar and cream in his cold consommé.

Jefferson Davis, it was said, knew more of etiquette in a minute than Lincoln knew all his life.

The capture of Sumter united the North and unified the South. It made 'war Democrats' —i.e., Democrats who had voted against Lincoln—join him in the prosecution of the war. More United States property was cheerfully appropriated by the Confederacy, which showed that it was alive and kicking from the very first minute it was born.

Confederate troops were sent into Virginia and threatened the Capitol at Washington, and would have taken it if the city had not, in summer, been regarded as unhealthful.

The Sixth Massachusetts Regiment, hurrying to the capital, was attacked in Baltimore and several men were killed. This was the first actual bloodshed in the civil war which caused rivers and lakes and torrents of the best blood of North and South to cover the fair, sweet clover fields and blue-grass meadows made alone for peace.

The general opinion of the author, thirty-five years afterwards, is that the war was as unavoidable as the deluge, and as idiotic in its incipiency as Adam's justly celebrated defence in the great 'Apple Sass Case.'

Men will fight until it is educated out of them, just as they will no doubt retain rudimentary tails and live in trees till they know better. It's all owing to how a man was brought up.

Of course after we have been drawn into the fight and been fined and sent home, we like to maintain that we were fighting for our home, or liberty, or the flag, or something of the kind. We hate to admit that, as a nation, we fought and paid for it afterwards with our family's bread-money just because we were irritated. That's natural; but most great wars are arranged by people who stay at home and sell groceries to the widow and orphan and old maids at one hundred per cent. advance.

Arlington Heights and Alexandria were now seized and occupied by the Union troops for the protection of Washington, and mosquito-wires were put up in the Capitol windows to keep the largest of the rebels from coming in and biting Congress.

Fort Monroe was garrisoned by a force under General Benjamin F. Butler, and an expedition was sent out against Big Bethel. On the way the Federal troops fired into each other, which pleased the Confederates very much indeed. The Union troops were repulsed with loss, and went back to the fort, where they stated that they were disappointed in the war.

West Virginia was strongly for the Union in sentiment, and was set off from the original State of Virginia, and, after some fighting the first year of the war over its territory, came into line with the Northern States. The fighting here was not severe. Generals McClellan and Rosecrans (Union) and Lee (Confederate) were the principal commanders.

The first year of the war was largely spent in sparring for wind, as one very able authority has it.

In the next chapter reference will be made to the battle of Bull Run, and the odium will be placed where it belongs. The author reluctantly closes this chapter in order to go out and get some odium for that purpose.

CHAPTER XXV.

BULL RUN AND OTHER BATTLES.

On the 21st of July, 1861, occurred the battle of Bull Run, under the joint management of General Irwin McDowell and General P. G. T. Beauregard. After a sharp conflict, the Confederates were repulsed, but rallied again under General T. J. Jackson, called thereafter Stonewall Jackson. While the Federals were striving to beat Jackson back, troops under Generals Early and Kirby Smith from Manassas Junction were hurled against their flank.[5] McDowell's men retreated, and as they reached the bridge a shell burst among their crowded and chaotic numbers. A caisson was upset, and a panic ensued, many of the troops continuing at a swift canter till they reached the Capitol, where they could call on the sergeant-at-arms to preserve order.

As a result of this run on the banks of the Potomac, the North suddenly decided that the war might last a week or two longer than at first stated, that the foe could not be killed with cornstalks, and that a mistake had been made in judging that the rebellion wasn't loaded.[6] Half a million men were called for and five hundred million dollars voted. General George B. McClellan took command of the Army of the Potomac.

The battle of Ball's Bluff resulted disastrously to the Union forces, and two thousand men were mostly driven into the Potomac, some drowned and others shot. Colonel Baker, United States Senator from Oregon, was killed.

The war in Missouri now opened. Captain Lyon reserved the United States arsenal at St. Louis, and defeated Colonel Marmaduke at Booneville. General Sigel was defeated at Carthage, July 5, by the Confederates: so Lyon, with five thousand men, decided to attack more than twice that number of the enemy under Price and McCulloch, which he did, August 10, at Wilson's Creek. He was killed while making a charge, and his men were defeated.

General Frémont then took command, and drove Price to Springfield, but he was in a short time replaced by General Hunter, because his war policy was offensive to the enemy. Hunter was soon afterwards removed, and Major-General Halleck took his place. Halleck gave general satisfaction to the enemy, and even his red messages from Washington, where he boarded during the war, were filled with nothing but kindness for the misguided foe.

Davis early in the war commissioned privateers, and Lincoln blockaded the Southern ports. The North had but one good vessel at the time, and those who have tried to blockade four or five thousand miles of hostile coast with one vessel know full well what it is to be busy. The entire navy consisted of forty-two ships, and some of these were not seaworthy. Some of them were so pervious that their guns had to be tied on to keep them from leaking through the cracks of the vessel.

Hatteras Inlet was captured, and Commodore Dupont, aided by General Thomas W. Sherman, captured Port Royal Entrance and Tybee Island. Port Royal became the dépôt for the fleet.

It was now decided at the South to send Messrs. Mason and Slidell to England, partly for change of scene and rest, and partly to make a friendly call on Queen Victoria and invite her to come and spend the season at Asheville, North Carolina. It was also hoped that she would give a few readings from her own works at the South, while her retinue could go to the front and have fun with the Yankees, if so disposed.

These gentlemen, wearing their nice new broadcloth clothes, and with a court suit and suitable night-wear to use in case they should be pressed to stop a week or two at the castle, got to Havana safely, and took passage on the British ship Trent; but Captain Wilkes, of the United States steamer San Jacinto, took them off the Trent, just as Mr. Mason had drawn and fortunately filled a hand with which he hoped to pay a part of the war-debt of the South and get a new overcoat in London. Later, however, the United States disavowed this act of Captain Wilkes, and said it was only a bit of pleasantry on his part.

HOPED SHE WOULD GIVE A FEW READINGS FROM HER OWN
WORKS.

The first year of the war had taught both sides a few truths, and especially that the war did not in any essential features resemble a straw-ride to camp-meeting and return. The South had also discovered that the Yankee peddlers could not be captured with fly-paper, and that although war was not their regular job they were willing to learn how it was done.

In 1862 the national army numbered five hundred thousand men, and the Confederate army three hundred and fifty thousand. Three objects were decided upon by the Federal government for the Union army and navy to accomplish,—viz., 1, the opening of the Mississippi; 2, the blockade of Southern ports; and 3, the capture of Richmond, the capital of the Southern Confederacy.

The capture of Forts Henry and Donelson was undertaken by General Grant, aided by Commodore Foote, and on February 6 a bombardment was opened with great success, reducing Fort Henry in one hour. The garrison got away because the land-forces had no idea the fort would yield so soon, and therefore could not get up there in time to cut off the retreat.

Fort Donelson was next attacked, the garrison having been reinforced by the men from Fort Henry. The fight lasted four days, and on February 16 the fort, with fifteen thousand men, surrendered.

Nashville was now easily occupied by Buell, and Columbus and Bowling Green were taken. The Confederates fell back to Corinth, where General Beauregard (Peter G. T.) and Albert Sidney Johnston massed their forces.

General Grant now captured the Memphis and Charleston Railroad; but the Confederates decided to capture him before Buell, who had been ordered to reinforce him, should effect a junction with him. April 6 and 7, therefore, the battle of Shiloh occurred. Whether the Union troops were surprised or not at this battle, we cannot here pause to discuss. Suffice it to say that one of the Federal officers admitted to the author in 1879, while under the influence of koumys, that, though not strictly surprised, he believed he violated no confidence in saying that they were somewhat astonished.

It was Sunday morning, and the Northern hordes were just considering whether they would take a bite of beans and go to church or remain in camp and get their laundry-work counted for Monday, when the Confederacy and some other men burst upon them with a fierce, rude yell. In a few moments the Federal troops had decided that there had sprung up a strong personal enmity on the part of the South, and that ill feeling had been engendered in some way.

All that beautiful Sabbath-day they fought, the Federals yielding ground slowly and reluctantly till the bank of the river was reached and Grant's artillery commanded the position. Here a stand was made until Buell came up, and shortly afterwards the Confederates fell back; but they had captured the Yankee camp entire, and many a boy in blue lost the nice warm woollen pulse-warmers crocheted for him by his soul's idol. It is said that over thirty-five hundred needle-books and three thousand men were captured by the Confederates, also thirty flags and immense quantities of stores; but the Confederate commander, General A. S. Johnston, was killed. The following morning the tide had turned, and General P. G. T. Beauregard retreated unmolested to Corinth.

SOME OTHER MEN BURST UPON THEM WITH A FIERCE, RUDE YELL.

General Halleck now took command, and, as the Confederates went away from there, he occupied Corinth, though still retaining his rooms at the Arlington Hotel in Washington.

The Confederates who retreated from Columbus fell back to Island No. 10 in the Mississippi River, where Commodore Foote bombarded them for three weeks, thus purifying the air and making the enemy feel much better than at any previous time during the campaign. General Pope crossed the Mississippi, capturing the batteries in the rear of the island, and turning them on the enemy, who surrendered April 7, the day of the battle of Shiloh.

May 10, the Union gun-boats moved down the river. Fort Pillow was abandoned by the Southern forces, and the Confederate flotilla was destroyed in front of Memphis. Kentucky and Tennessee were at last the property of the fierce hordes from the great coarse North.

General Bragg was now at Chattanooga, Price at Iuka, and Van Dorn at Holly Springs. All these generals had guns, and were at enmity with the United States of America. They very much desired to break the Union line of investment extending from Memphis almost to Chattanooga.

Bragg started out for the Ohio River, intending to cross it and capture the Middle States; but Buell heard of it and got there twenty-four hours ahead, wherefore Bragg abandoned his plans, as it flashed over him like a clap of thunder from a clear sky that he had no place to put the Middle States if he had them. He therefore escaped in the darkness, his wagon-trains sort of drawling over forty miles of road and 'hit a-rainin'.'

September 19, General Price, who, with Van Dorn, had considered it a good time to attack Grant, who had sent many troops north to prevent Bragg's capture of North America, decided to retreat, and, General Rosecrans failing to cut him off, escaped, and was thus enabled to fight on other occasions.

The two Confederate generals now decided to attack the Union forces at Corinth, which they did. They fought beautifully, especially the Texan and Missouri troops, who did some heroic work, but they were defeated and driven forty miles with heavy loss.

October 30, General Buell was succeeded by General Rosecrans.

The battle of Murfreesboro occurred December 31 and January 2. It was one of the bloodiest battles of the whole conflict, and must have made the men who brought on the war by act of Congress feel first-rate. About one-fourth of those engaged were killed.

An attack on Vicksburg, in which Grant and Sherman were to co-operate, the former moving along the Mississippi Central Railroad and Sherman descending the river from Memphis, was disastrous, and the capture of Arkansas Post, January 11, 1863, closed the campaign of 1862 on the Father of Waters.

General Price was driven out of Missouri by General Curtis, and had to stay in Arkansas quite a while, though he preferred a dryer climate.

General Van Dorn now took command of these forces, numbering twenty thousand men, and at Pea Ridge, March 7 and 8, 1863, he was defeated to a remarkable degree. During his retreat he could hardly restrain his impatience.

WENT HOME BEFORE THE EXERCISES WERE MORE THAN HALF THROUGH.

Some four or five thousand Indians joined the Confederates in this battle, but were so astonished at the cannon, and so shocked by the large decayed balls, as they called the shells, which came hurtling through the air, now and then hurting an Indian severely, that they went home before the exercises were more than half through. They were down on the programme for some fantastic and interesting tortures of Union prisoners, but when they got home to the reservation and had picked the briers out of themselves they said that war was about as barbarous a thing as they were ever to, and they went to bed early, leaving a call for 9.30 A.M. on the following day.

The red brother's style of warfare has an air about it that is unpopular now. A common stone stab-knife is a feeble thing to use against people who shoot a distance of eight miles with a gun that carries a forty-gallon caldron full of red-hot iron.

CHAPTER XXVI.

SOME MORE FRATRICIDAL STRIFE.

The effort to open the Mississippi from the north was seconded by an expedition from the south, in which Captain David G. Farragut, commanding a fleet of forty vessels, co-operated with General Benjamin F. Butler, with the capture of New Orleans as the object.

Mortar-boats covered with green branches for the purpose of fooling the enemy, as no one could tell at any distance at all whether these were or were not olive-branches, steamed up the river and bombarded Forts Jackson and St. Philip till the stunned catfish rose to the surface of the water to inquire, 'Why all this?' and turned their pallid stomachs toward the soft Southern zenith. Sixteen thousand eight hundred shells were thrown into the two forts, but that did not capture New Orleans.

Farragut now decided to run his fleet past the defences, and, desperate as the chances were, he started on April 24. A big cable stretched across the river suggested the idea that there was a hostile feeling among the New Orleans people. Five rafts and armed steamers met him, and the iron-plated ram Manassas extended to him a cordial welcome to a wide wet grave with a southern exposure.

Farragut cut through the cable about three o'clock in the morning, practically destroyed the Confederate fleet, and steamed up to the city, which was at his mercy.

The forts, now threatened in the rear by Butler's army, surrendered, and Farragut went up to Baton Rouge and took possession of it. General Butler's occupation at New Orleans has been variously commented upon by both friend and foe, but we are only able to learn from this and the entire record of the war, in fact, that it is better to avoid hostilities unless one is ready to accept the unpleasant features of combat. The author, when a boy, learned this after he had acquired the unpleasant features resulting from combat which the artist has cleverly shown on opposite page.

General Butler said he found it almost impossible to avoid giving offence to the foe, and finally he gave it up in despair.

The French are said to be the politest people on the face of the earth, but no German will admit it; and though the Germans are known to have big, warm, hospitable hearts, since the Franco-Prussian war you couldn't get a Frenchman to admit this.

In February Burnside captured Roanoke Island, and the coast of North Carolina fell into the hands of the Union army. Port Royal became the base of operations against Florida, and at the close of the year 1862 every city on the Atlantic coast except Charleston, Wilmington, and Savannah was held by the Union army.

UNPLEASANT FEATURES RESULTING
FROM COMBAT.

The Merrimac iron-clad, which had made much trouble for the Union shipping for some time, steamed into Hampton Roads on the 8th of March. Hampton Roads is not the Champs-Elysées of the South, but a long wet stretch of track east of Virginia, — the Midway Plaisance of the Salted Sea. The Merrimac steered for the Cumberland, rammed her, and the Cumberland sunk like a stove-lid, with all on board. The captain of the Congress, warned by the fate of the Cumberland, ran his vessel on shore and tried to conceal her behind the tall grass, but the Merrimac followed and shelled her till she surrendered.

The Merrimac then went back to Norfolk, where she boarded, night having come on apace. In the morning she aimed to clear out the balance of the Union fleet. That night, however, the Monitor, a flat little craft with a revolving tower, invented by Captain Ericsson, arrived, and in the morning when the Merrimac started in on her day's work of devastation, beginning with the Minnesota, the insignificant-looking Monitor slid up to the iron monster and gave her two one-hundred-and-sixty-six-and-three-quarter-pound solid shot.

The Merrimac replied with a style of broadside that generally sunk her adversary, but the balls rolled off the low flat deck and fell with a solemn plunk in the moaning sea, or broke in fragments and lay on the forward deck like the shells of antique eggs on the floor of the House of Parliament after a Home Rule argument.

Five times the Merrimac tried to ram the little spitz-pup of the navy, but her huge iron beak rode up over the slippery deck of the enemy, and when the big vessel looked over her sides to see its wreck, she discovered that the Monitor was right side up and ready for more.

The Confederate vessel gave it up at last, and went back to Norfolk defeated, her career suddenly closed by the timely genius of the able Scandinavian.

The Peninsular campaign was principally addressed toward the capture of Richmond. One hundred thousand men were massed at Fort Monroe April 4, and marched slowly toward Yorktown, where five thousand Confederates under General Magruder stopped the great army under McClellan.

After a month's siege, and just as McClellan was about to shoot at the town, the garrison took its valise and went away.

On the 5th of May occurred the battle of Williamsburg, between the forces under 'Fighting Joe' Hooker and General Johnston. It lasted nine hours, and ended in the routing of the Confederates and their pursuit by Hooker to within seven miles of Richmond. This caused the adjournment of the Confederate Congress.

But Johnston prevented the junction of McDowell and McClellan after the capture of Hanover Court-House, and Stonewall Jackson, reinforced by Ewell, scared the Union forces almost to death. They crossed the Potomac, having marched thirty-five miles per day. Washington was getting too hot now to hold people who could get away.

It was hard to say which capital had been scared the worst.

The Governors of the Northern States were asked to send militia to defend the capital, and the front door of the White House was locked every night after ten o'clock.

But finally the Union generals, instead of calling for more troops, got after General Jackson, and he fled from the Shenandoah Valley, burning the bridges behind him. It is said that as he and his staff were about to cross their last bridge they saw a mounted gun on the opposite side, manned by a Union artilleryman. Jackson rode up and in clarion tones called out, 'Who told you to put that gun there, sir? Bring it over here, sir, and mount it, and report at head-quarters this evening, sir!' The artilleryman unlimbered the gun, and while he was placing it General Jackson and staff crossed over and joined the army.

One cannot be too careful, during a war, in the matter of obedience to orders. We should always know as nearly as possible whether our orders come from the proper authority or not.

No one can help admiring this dashing officer's tour in the Shenandoah Valley, where he kept three major-generals and sixty thousand troops awake nights with fifteen thousand men, saved Richmond, scared Washington into fits, and prevented the union of McClellan's and McDowell's forces. Had there been more such men, and a little more confidence in the great volume of typographical errors called Confederate money, the lovely character who pens these lines might have had a different tale to tell.

May 31 and June 1 occurred the battle of Fair Oaks, where McClellan's men floundering in the mud of the Chickahominy swamps were pounced upon by General Johnston, who was wounded the first day. On the following day, as a result of this accident, Johnston's men were repulsed in disorder.

General Robert E. Lee, who was now in command of the Confederate forces, desired to make his army even more offensive than it had been, and on June 12 General Stuart led off with his cavalry, made the entire circuit of the Union army, saw how it looked from behind, and returned to Richmond, much improved in health, having had several meals of victuals while absent.

Hooker now marched to where he could see the dome of the court-house at Richmond, but just then McClellan heard that Jackson had been seen in the neighborhood of Hanover Court-House, and so decided to change his base. General McClellan was a man of great refinement, and would never use the same base over a week at a time.

He had hardly got the base changed when Lee fell upon his flank at Mechanicsville, June 26, and the Seven Days' battle followed. The Union troops fought and fell back, fought and fell back, until Malvern Hill was reached, where, worn with marching, choked with dust, and broken down by the heat, to which they were unaccustomed, they made their last stand, July 1. Here Lee got such a reception that he did not insist on going any farther.

But the Union army was cooped up on the James River. The siege of Richmond had been abandoned, and the North felt blue and discouraged. Three hundred thousand more men were called for, and it seemed that, as in the South, 'the cradle and the grave were to be robbed' for more troops.

Lee now decided to take Washington and butcher Congress to make a Roman holiday. General Pope met the Confederates August 26, and while Lee and Jackson were separated could have whipped the latter had the Army of the Potomac reinforced him as it should, but, full of malaria and foot-sore with marching, it did not reach him in time, and Pope had to fight the entire Confederate army on that historic ground covered with so many unpleasant memories and other things, called Bull Run.

WHERE BEER WAS ONLY FIVE CENTS PER GLASS.

For the second time the worn and wilted Union army was glad to get back to Washington, where the President was, and where beer was only five cents per glass.

Oh, how sad everything seemed at that time to the North, and how high cotton cloth was! The bride who hastily married her dear one and bade him good-by as the bugle called him to the war, pointed with pride to her cotton clothes as a mark of wealth; and the middle classes were only too glad to have a little cotton mixed with their woollen clothes.

Lee invaded Maryland, and McClellan, restored to command of the Army of the Potomac, followed him, and found a copy of his order of march, which revealed the fact that only a portion of the army was before him. So, overtaking the Confederates at South Mountain, he was ready for a victory, but waited one day; and in the mountains

Lee got his troops united again, while Jackson also returned. The Union troops had over eighty thousand in their ranks, and nothing could have been more thoughtful or genteel than to wait for the Confederates to get as many together as possible, otherwise the battle might have been brief and unsatisfactory to the tax-payer or newspaper subscriber, who of course wants his money's worth when he pays for a battle. WANTS HIS MONEY'S WORTH WHEN HE PAYS FOR A BATTLE.

The battle of Antietam was a very fierce one, and undecisive, yet it saved Washington from an invasion by the Confederates, who would have done a good deal of trading there, no doubt, entirely on credit, thus injuring business very much and loading down Washington merchants with book accounts, which, added to what they had charged already to members of Congress, would have made times in Washington extremely dull.

General McClellan, having impressed the country with the idea that he was a good bridge- builder, but a little too dilatory in the matter of carnage, was succeeded by General Burnside.

President Lincoln had written the Proclamation of Emancipation to the slaves in July, but waited for a victory before publishing it. Bull Run as a victory was not up to his standard; so when Lee was driven from Maryland the document was issued by which all slaves in the United States became free; and, although thirty-one years have passed at this writing, they are still dropping in occasionally from the back districts to inquire about the truth of the report.

STILL DROPPING IN OCCASIONALLY FROM THE BACK
DISTRICTS.

CHAPTER XXVII.

STILL MORE FRATERNAL BLOODSHED, ON PRINCIPLE.—
OUTING FEATURES DISAPPEAR, AND GIVE PLACE TO
STRAINED RELATIONS BETWEEN COMBATANTS, WHO BEGIN
TO MIX THINGS.

On December 13 the year's business closed with the battle of
Fredericksburg, under the management of General Burnside. Twelve
thousand Union troops were killed before night mercifully shut
down upon the slaughter.

The Confederates were protected by stone walls and situated upon a
commanding height, from which they were able to shoot down the
Yankees with perfect sang-froid and deliberation.

In the midst of all these discouragements, the red brother fetched loose in Minnesota, Iowa, and Dakota, and massacred seven hundred men, women, and children. The outbreak was under the management of Little Crow, and was confined to the Sioux Nation. Thirty-nine of these Indians were hanged on the same scaffold at Mankato, Minnesota, as a result of this wholesale murder.

This execution constitutes one of the green spots in the author's memory. In all lives now and then an oasis is liable to fall. This was oasis enough to last the writer for years.

In 1863 the Federal army numbered about seven hundred thousand men, and the Confederates about three hundred and fifty thousand. Still it took two more years to close the war.

It is held now by good judges that the war was prolonged by the jealousy existing between Union commanders who wanted to be President or something else, and that it took so much time for the generals to keep their eyes on caucuses and county papers at home that they fought best when surprised and attacked by the foe.

General Grant moved again on Vicksburg, and on May 1, defeated Pemberton at Fort Gibson. He also prevented a junction between Joseph E. Johnston and Pemberton, and drove the latter into Vicksburg, securing the stopper so tightly that after forty-seven days the garrison surrendered, July 4. This fight cost the Confederates thirty-seven thousand prisoners, ten thousand killed and wounded, and immense quantities of stores. It was a warm time in Vicksburg; a curious man who stuck his hat out for twenty seconds above the ramparts found fifteen bullet-holes in it when he took it down, and when he wore it to church he attracted more attention than the collection.

The North now began to sit up and take notice. Morning papers began to sell once more, and Grant was the name on every tongue.

The Mississippi was open to the Gulf, and the Confederacy was practically surrounded.

ATTRACTED MORE ATTENTION THAN THE COLLECTION.

Rosecrans would have moved on the enemy, but learned that the foe had several head of cavalry more than he did, also a team of artillery. At this time John Morgan made a raid into Ohio. He surrounded Cincinnati, but did not take it, as he was not keeping house at the time and hated to pay storage on it. He got to Parkersburg, West Virginia, and was captured there with almost his entire force.

On September 19 and 20 occurred the battle of Chickamauga. Longstreet rushed into a breach in the Union line and swept it with a great big besom of wrath with which he had wisely provided himself on starting out. Rosecrans felt mortified when he came to himself and found that his horse had been so unmanageable that he had carried him ten miles from the carnage.

But the left, under Thomas, held fast its position, and no doubt saved the little band of sixty thousand men which Rosecrans commanded at the time.

His army now found itself shut up in intrenchments, with Bragg on the hills threatening the Union forces with starvation.

On November 24-25 a battle near Chattanooga took place, with Grant at the head of the Federal forces. Hooker came to join him from the Army of the Potomac, and Sherman hurried to his standard from Iuka. Thomas made a dash and captured Orchard Knob, and Hooker, on the following day, charged Lookout Mountain.

This was the most brilliant, perhaps, of Grant's victories. It is known as the 'battle of Missionary Ridge.' Hooker had exceeded his prerogative and kept on after capturing the crest of Lookout Mountain, while Sherman was giving the foe several varieties of fits, from the north, when Grant discovered that before him the line was being weakened in order to help the Confederate flanks. So with Thomas he crossed through the first line and over the rifle-pits, forgot that he had intended to halt and reform, and concluded to wait and reform after the war was over, when he should have more time, and that night along the entire line of heights the camp-fires of the Union army winked at one another in ghoulish glee.

The army under Bragg was routed, and Bragg resigned his command.

Burnside, who had been relieved of the command of the Army of the Potomac, was sent to East Tennessee, where the brave but frost-bitten troops of Longstreet shut him up at Knoxville and compelled him to board at the railroad eating-house there.

Sherman's worn and weary boys were now ordered at once to the relief of Burnside, and Longstreet, getting word of it, made a furious assault on the former, who repulsed him with loss, and he went away from there as Sherman approached from the west.

'WHERE AM I?'

Hooker had succeeded Burnside in the command of the Army of the Potomac, and he judged that, as Lee was now left with but sixty thousand men, while the Army of the Potomac contained one hundred thousand who craved out-of-door exercise, he might do well to go and get Lee, returning in the cool of the evening. Lee, however, accomplished the division of his army while concealed in the woods and sent Jackson to fall on Hooker's rear. The close of the fight found Hooker on his old camping-ground opposite Fredericksburg, murmuring to himself, in a dazed sort of way,

'Where am I?' Lee felt so good over this that he decided to go North and get something to eat. He also decided to get catalogues and price-lists of Philadelphia and New York while there. Threatening Baltimore in order to mislead General Meade, who was now in command of the Federals, Lee struck into Pennsylvania and met with the Union cavalry a little west of Gettysburg on the Chambersburg road. It is said that Gettysburg was not intended by either army as the site for the battle, Lee hoping to avoid a fight, depending as he did on the well-known hospitality of the Pennsylvanians, and Meade intending to have the fight at Pipe Creek, where he had some property.

July 1-2-3 were the dates of this memorable battle. The first day was rather favorable to Lee, quite a number of Yankee prisoners being taken while they were lost in the crowded streets of Gettysburg.

The second day was opened by Longstreet, who charged the Union left, and ran across Sickles, who had by mistake formed in the way of Meade's intended line of battle. They outflanked him, but, as they swung around him, Warren met them with a diabolical welcome, which stayed them. Sickles found himself on Cemetery Ridge, while the Confederates under Ewell were on Culp's Hill.

On the third day, at one P.M., Lee opened with one hundred and fifty guns on Cemetery Ridge. The air was a hornet's nest of screaming shells with fiery tails. As it lulled a little, out of the woods came eighteen thousand men in battle-array extending over a mile in length. The Yankees knew a good thing when they saw it, and they paused to admire this beautiful gathering of foemen in whose veins there flowed the same blood as in their own, and whose ancestors had stood shoulder to shoulder with their own in a hundred battles for freedom.

Their sentiment gave place to shouts of battle, and into the silent phalanx a hundred guns poured their red-hot messages of death. The golden grain was drenched with the blood of men no less brave because they were not victorious, and the rich fields of Pennsylvania drank with thirsty eagerness the warm blood of many a Southern son.

Yet they moved onward. Volley after volley of musketry mowed them down, and the puny reaper in the neglected grain gave place to the grim reaper Death, all down that unwavering line of gray and brown.

They marched up to the Union breastworks, bayoneted the gunners at their work, planted their flags on the parapets, and, while the Federals converged from every point to this, exploding powder burned the faces of these contending hosts, who, hand to hand, fought each other to death, while far-away widows and orphans multiplied to mourn through the coming years over this ghastly folly of civil war.

Whole companies of the Confederates rushed as prisoners into the arms of their enemies, and the shattered remnant of the battered foe retreated from the field.

While all this was going on in Pennsylvania, Pemberton was arranging terms of surrender at Vicksburg, and from this date onward the Confederacy began to wobble in its orbit, and the President of this ill-advised but bitterly punished scheme began to wish that he had been in Canada when the war broke out.

In April of the same year Admiral Dupont, an able seaman with massive whiskers, decided to run the fortifications at Charleston with iron-clads, but the Charleston people thought they could run them themselves. So they drove him back after the sinking of the Kennebec and the serious injury of all the other vessels.

General Gillmore then landed with troops. Fort Wagner was captured. The 54th Regiment of colored troops, the finest organized in the Free States, took a prominent part and fought with great coolness and bravery. By December there were fifty thousand colored troops enlisted, and before the war closed over two hundred thousand.

PRICE OF LIVING RUNNING
UP TO EIGHT HUNDRED AND NINE
HUNDRED DOLLARS PER DAY.

It is needless to say that this made the Yankee unpopular at the time in the best society of the South.

General Gillmore attempted to capture Sumter, and did reduce it to a pulp, but when he went to gather it he was met by a garrison still concealed in the basement, and peppered with volleys of hot shingle-nails and other bric-à-brac, which forced him to retire with loss.

He said afterward that Fort Sumter was not desirable anyhow.

This closed the most memorable year of the war, with the price of living at the South running up to eight hundred and nine hundred dollars per day, and currency depreciating so rapidly that one's salary had to be advanced every morning in order to keep pace with the price of mule-steaks.

CHAPTER XXVIII.

LAST YEAR OF THE DISAGREEABLE WAR.

General Grant was now in command of all the Union troops, and in 1864-5 the plan of operation was to prevent the junction of the Confederates,—General Grant seeking to interest the army in Virginia under General Lee, and General Sherman the army of General Joseph E. Johnston in Georgia.

Sherman started at once, and came upon Johnston located on almost impregnable hills all the way to Atlanta. The battles of Dalton, Resaca, Dallas, Lost Mountain, and Kenesaw Mountain preceded Johnston's retreat to the intrenchments of Atlanta, July 10, Sherman having been on the move since early in May, 1864.

Jefferson Davis, disgusted with Johnston, placed Hood in command, who made three heroic attacks upon the Union troops, but was repulsed. Sherman now gathered fifteen days' rations from the neighbors, and, throwing his forces across Hood's line of supplies, compelled him to evacuate the city.

The historian says that Sherman was entirely supplied from Nashville *via* railroad during this trip, but the author knows of his own personal knowledge that there were times when he got his fresh provisions along the road.

This expedition cost the Union army thirty thousand men and the Confederates thirty-five thousand. Besides, Georgia was the Confederacy, so far as arms, grain, etc., were concerned. Sherman attributed much of his success to the fact that he could repair and operate the railroad so rapidly. Among his men were Yankee machinists and engineers, who were as necessary as courageous fighters.

'We are held here during many priceless hours,' said the general, 'because the enemy has spoiled this passenger engine. Who knows any thing about repairing an engine?'

GETTING FRESH PROVISIONS ALONG THE ROAD.

'I do,' said a dusty tramp in blue. 'I can repair this one in an hour.'

'What makes you think so?'

'Well, I made it.'

This was one of the strong features of Sherman's army. Among the hundred thousand who composed it there were so many active brains and skilled hands that the toot of the engine caught the heels of the last echoing shout of the battle.

Learning that Hood proposed to invade Tennessee, Sherman prepared to march across Georgia to the sea, and if necessary to tramp through the Atlantic States.

Hood was sorry afterwards that he invaded Tennessee. He shut Thomas up in Nashville after a battle with Schofield, and kept the former in-doors for two weeks, when all of a sudden Thomas exclaimed, 'Air! air! give me air!' and came out, throwing Hood into headlong flight, when the Union cavalry fell on his rear, followed by the infantry, and the forty thousand Confederates became a scattered and discouraged mob spread out over several counties.

The burning of Atlanta preceded Sherman's march, and, though one of the saddest features of the war, was believed to be a military necessity. Those who declare war hoping to have a summer's outing thereby may live to regret it for many bitter years.

On November 16, Sherman started, his army moving in four columns, constituting altogether a column of fire by night, and a pillar of cloud and dust by day. Kilpatrick's cavalry scoured the country like a mass meeting of ubiquitous little black Tennessee hornets.

In five weeks Sherman had marched three hundred miles, had destroyed two railroads, had stormed Fort McAllister, and had captured Savannah.

On the 5th and 6th of May, 1864, occurred the battle of the Wilderness, near the old battleground of Chancellorsville. No one could describe it, for it was fought in the dense woods, and the two days of useless butchery with not the slightest signs of civilized warfare sickened both armies, and, with no victory for either, they retired to their intrenchments.

Grant, instead of retreating, however, quietly passed the flank of the Confederates and started for Spottsylvania Court-House, where a battle occurred May 8-12.

Here the two armies fought five days without any advantage to either. It was at this time that Grant sent his celebrated despatch stating that he 'proposed to fight it out on this line if it took all summer.'

Finally he sought to turn Lee's right flank. June 8, the battle of Cold Harbor followed this movement. The Union forces were shot down in the mire and brush by Lee's troops, now snugly in out of the wet, behind the Cold Harbor defences. One historian says that in twenty minutes ten thousand Yankee troops were killed; though Badeau, whose accuracy in counting dead has always been perfectly marvellous, admits only seven thousand in all.

Grant now turned his attention towards Petersburg, but Lee was there before him and intrenched, so the Union army had to intrench. This only postponed the evil day, however.

Things now shaped themselves into a siege of Richmond, with Petersburg as the first outpost of the besieged capital.

On the 30th of July, eight thousand pounds of powder were carefully inserted under a Confederate fort and the entire thing hoisted in the air, leaving a huge hole, in which, a few hours afterwards, many a boy in blue met his death, for in the assault which followed the explosion the Union soldiers were mowed down by the concentrated fire of the Confederates. The Federals threw away four thousand lives here.

On the 18th of August the Weldon Railroad was captured, which was a great advantage to Grant, and, though several efforts were made to recapture it, they were unsuccessful.

General Early was delegated to threaten Washington and scare the able officers of the army who were stopping there at that time talking politics and abusing Grant. He defeated General Wallace at Monocacy River, and appeared before Fort Stevens, one of the defences of Washington, July 11. Had he whooped right along instead of pausing a day somewhere to get laundry-work done before entering Washington, he would easily have captured the city.

Reinforcements, however, got there ahead of him, and he had to go back. He sent a force of cavalry into Pennsylvania, where they captured Chambersburg and burned it on failure of the town trustees to pay five hundred thousand dollars ransom.

General Sheridan was placed in charge of the troops here, and defeated Early at Winchester, riding twenty miles in twenty minutes, as per poem. At Fisher's Hill he was also victorious. He devastated the Valley of the Shenandoah to such a degree that a crow passing the entire length of the valley had to carry his dinner with him.

PAUSING TO GET LAUNDRY-WORK DONE.

It was, however, at the battle of Cedar Creek that Sheridan was twenty miles away, according to historical prose. Why he was twenty miles away, various and conflicting reasons are given, but on his good horse Rienzi he arrived in time to turn defeat and rout into victory and hilarity.

Rienzi, after the war, died in eleven States. He was a black horse, with a saddle-gall and a flashing eye.

He passed away at his home in Chicago at last in poverty while waiting for a pension applied for on the grounds of founder and lampers brought on by eating too heartily after the battle and while warm, but in the line of duty.

The Red River campaign under General Banks was a joint naval and land expedition, resulting in the capture of Fort de Russy, March 14, after which, April 8, the troops marching towards Shreveport in very open order, single file or holding one another's hands and singing 'John Brown's Body,' were attacked by General Dick Taylor, and if Washington had not been so far away and through a hostile country, Bull Run would have had another rival. But the boys rallied, and next day repulsed the Confederates, after which they returned to New Orleans, where board was more reasonable. General Banks obtained quite a relief at this time: he was relieved of his command.

August 5, Commodore Farragut captured Mobile, after a neat and attractive naval fight, and on the 24th and 25th of December Commodore Porter and General Butler started out to take Fort Fisher. After two days' bombardment, Butler decided that there were other forts to be had on better terms, and returned. Afterwards General Terry commanded the second expedition, Porter having remained on hand with his vessels to assist. January 15, 1865, the most heroic fighting on both sides resulted, and at last, completely hemmed in, the brave and battered garrison surrendered; but no one who was there need blush to say so, even to-day.

At the South at this time coffee was fifty dollars a pound and gloves were one hundred and fifty dollars a pair. Flour was forty dollars a barrel; but you could get a barrel of currency for less than that.

Money was plenty, but what was needed seemed to be confidence. Running the blockade was not profitable at that time, since over fifteen hundred head of Confederate vessels were captured during the war.

The capture of Fort Fisher closed the last port of the South, and left the Confederacy no show with foreign Powers or markets.

The Alabama was an armed steam-ship, and the most unpleasant feature of the war to the Federal government, especially as she had more sympathy and aid in England than was asked for or expected by the Unionists. However, England has since repaid all this loss in various ways. She has put from five to eight million dollars into cattle on the plains of the Northwest, where the skeletons of same may be found bleaching in the summer sun; and I am personally acquainted with six Americans now visiting England who can borrow enough in a year to make up all the losses sustained through the Alabama and other neutral vessels.

PERSONALLY ACQUAINTED WITH SIX AMERICANS.

Captain Semmes commanded the Alabama, and off Cherbourg he sent a challenge to the Kearsarge, commanded by Captain Winslow, who accepted it, and so worked his vessel that the Alabama had to move round him in a circle, while he filled her up with iron, lead, copper, tin, German silver, glass, nails, putty, paint, varnishes, and dye-stuff. At the seventh rotation the Alabama ran up the white flag and sunk with a low mellow plunk. The crew was rescued by Captain Winslow and the English yacht Deerhound, the latter taking Semmes and starting for England.

This matter, however, was settled in after-years.

The care of the sick, the dying, and the dead in the Union armies was almost entirely under the eye of the merciful and charitable, loyal and loving members of the Sanitary and ChristianCommissions, whose work and its memory kept green in the hearts of the survivors and their children will be monument enough for the coming centuries.

In July, 1864, the debt of the country was two billion dollars and twenty cents. Two dollars and ninety cents in greenbacks would buy a reluctant gold dollar.

Still, Abraham Lincoln was re-elected against George B. McClellan, the Democratic candidate, who carried only three States. This was endorsement enough for the policy of President Lincoln.

Sherman's army of sixty thousand, after a month's rest at Savannah, started north to unite with Grant in the final blow. 'Before it was terror, behind it ashes.'

Columbia was captured February 17, and burned, without Sherman's authority, the night following. Charleston was evacuated the next day. Johnston was recalled to take command, and opposed the march of Sherman, but was driven back after fierce engagements at Bentonville and Averysboro. On March 25 Lee decided to attack Grant, and, while the latter was busy, get out of Richmond and join Johnston, but when this battle, known as the attack on Fort Steadman, was over, Grant's hold was tighter than ever.

Sheridan attacked Lee's rear with a heavy force, and at Five Forks, April 1, the surprised garrison was defeated with five thousand captured. The next day the entire Union army advanced, and the line of Confederate intrenchments was broken. On the following day Petersburg and Richmond were evacuated, but Mr. Davis was not there. He had gone away. Rather than meet General Grant and entertain him when there was no pie in the house, he and the Treasury had escaped from the haunts of man, wishing to commune with nature for a while. He was captured at Irwinsville, Georgia, under peculiar and rather amusing circumstances.

He was never punished, with the exception perhaps that he published a book and did not realize anything from it.

Lee fled to the westward, but was pursued by the triumphant Federals, especially by Sheridan, whose cavalry hung on his flanks day and night. Food failed the fleeing foe, and the young shoots of trees for food and the larger shoots of the artillery between meals were too much for that proud army, once so strong and confident.

Let us not dwell on the particulars.

As Sheridan planted his cavalry squarely across Lee's path of retreat, the worn but heroic tatters of a proud army prepared to sell themselves for a bloody ransom and go down fighting, but Grant had demanded their surrender, and, seeing back of the galling, skirmishing cavalry solid walls of confident infantry, the terms of surrender were accepted by General Lee, and April 9 the Confederate army stacked its arms near Appomattox Court-House.

The Confederate war debt was never paid, for some reason or other, but the Federal debt when it was feeling the best amounted to two billion eight hundred and forty-four million dollars. One million men lost their lives.

Was it worth while?

In the midst of the general rejoicing, President Lincoln was assassinated by John Wilkes Booth at Ford's Theatre, April 14. The assassin was captured in a dying condition in a burning barn, through a crack in the boarding of which he had been shot by a soldier named Boston Corbett. He died with no sympathetic applause to soothe the dull, cold ear of death.

West Virginia was admitted to the Union in 1863, and Nevada in 1864.

The following chapters will be devoted to more peaceful details, while we cheerfully close the sorrowful pages in which we have confessed that, with all our greatness as a nation, we could not stay the tide of war.

CHAPTER XXIX.

TOO MUCH LIBERTY IN PLACES AND NOT ENOUGH ELSEWHERE.—THOUGHTS ON THE LATE WAR—WHO IS THE BIGGER ASS, THE MAN WHO WILL NOT FORGIVE AND FORGET, OR THE MAWKISH AND MOIST-EYED SNIVELLER WHO WANTS TO DO THAT ALL THE TIME?

When Patrick Henry put his old cast-iron spectacles on the top of his head and whooped for liberty, he did not know that some day we should have more of it than we knew what to do with. He little dreamed that the time would come when we should have more liberty than we could pay for. When Mr. Henry sawed the air and shouted for liberty or death, I do not believe that he knew the time would come when Liberty would stand on Bedloe's Island and yearn for rest and change of scene.

It seems to me that we have too much liberty in this country in some ways. We have more liberty than we have money. We guarantee that every man in America shall fill himself up full of liberty at our expense, and the less of an American he is the more liberty he can have. Should he desire to enjoy himself, all he needs is a slight foreign accent and a willingness to mix up with politics as soon as he can get his baggage off the steamer. The more I study American institutions the more I regret that I was not born a foreigner, so that I could have something to say about the management of our great land. If I could not be a foreigner, I believe I should prefer to be a policeman or an Indian not taxed.

I am often led to ask, in the language of the poet, 'Is civilization a failure, and is the Caucasian played out?'

PATRICK HENRY'S GREAT SPEECH.

Almost every one can have a good deal of fun in America except the

American. He seems to be so busy paying his taxes that he has very little time to vote, or to mingle in society's giddy whirl, or to mix up with the nobility. That is the reason why the alien who rides across the United States in the 'Limited Mail' and writes a book about us before breakfast wonders why we are always in a hurry. That also is the reason why we have to throw our meals into ourselves with such despatch, and hardly have time to maintain a warm personal friendship with our families.

THE MORE I REGRET THAT I
WAS NOT BORN A FOREIGNER.

We do not care much for wealth, but we must have freedom, and freedom costs money. We have advertised to furnish a bunch of freedom to every man, woman, and child who comes to our shores, and we are going to deliver the goods whether we have any left for ourselves or not.

What would the great world beyond the seas say to us if some day the blue-eyed Oriental, with his heart full of love for our female seminaries and our old women's homes, should land upon our coasts and crave freedom in car-load lots but find that we were using all the liberty ourselves? But what do we want of liberty, anyhow? What could we do with it if we had it? It takes a man of leisure to enjoy liberty, and we have no leisure whatever. It is a good thing to keep in the house for the use of guests, but we don't need it for ourselves.

Therefore we have a statue of Liberty Enlightening the World, because it shows that we keep Liberty on tap winter and summer. We want the whole broad world to remember that when it gets tired of oppression it can come here to America and oppress us. We are used to it, and we rather like it. If we don't like it, we can get on the steamer and go abroad, where we may visit the effete monarchies and have a high old time.

The sight of the Goddess of Liberty standing there in New York harbor night and day, bathing her feet in the rippling sea, is a good thing. It is first-rate. It may also be productive of good in a direction that many have not thought of. As she stands there day after day, bathing her feet in the broad Atlantic, perhaps some moss-grown alien landing on our shore and moving toward the Far West may fix the bright picture in his so-called mind, and, remembering how, on his arrival in New York, he saw Liberty bathing her feet with impunity, he may be led in after-years to try it on himself.

More citizens and less voters will some day be adopted as the motto of the Republic.

One reference to the late war, and I will close. I want to refer especially to the chronic reconciler who when war was declared was not involved in it, but who now improves every opportunity, especially near election-time, to get out a tired olive-branch and make a tableau of himself. He is worse than the man who cannot forgive or forget.

The growth of reconciliation between the North and the South is the slow growth of years, and the work of generations. When any man, North or South, in a public place takes occasion to talk in a mellow and mawkish way of the great love he now has for his old enemy, watch him. He is getting ready to ask a favor. There is a beautiful, poetic idea in the reunion of two contending and shattered elements of a great nation. There is something beautifully pathetic in the picture of the North and the South clasped in each other's arms and shedding a torrent of hot tears down each other's backs as it is done in a play, but do you believe that the aged mothers on either side have learned to love the foe with much violence yet? Do you believe that the crippled veteran, North or South, now passionately loves the adversary who robbed him of his glorious youth, made him a feeble ruin, and mowed down his comrades with swift death? Do you believe that either warrior is so fickle that he has entirely deserted the cause for which he fought? Even the victor cannot ask that.

MAY BE LED TO TRY IT ON HIMSELF.

'Let the gentle finger of time undo, so far as may be, the devastation wrought by the war, and let succeeding generations seek through natural methods to reunite the business and the traffic that were interrupted by the war. Let the South guarantee to the Northern investor security to himself and his investment, and he will not ask for the love which we read of in speeches but do not expect and do not find in the South.

'Two warring parents on the verge of divorce have been saved the disgrace of separation and agreed to maintain their household for the sake of their children. Their love has been questioned by the world, and their relations strained. Is it not bad taste for them to pose in public and make a cheap Romeo and Juliet tableau of themselves?

'Let time and merciful silence obliterate the scars of war, and succeeding generations, fostered by the smiles of national prosperity, soften the bitterness of the past and mellow the memory of a mighty struggle in which each contending host called upon Almighty God to sustain the cause which it honestly believed to be just.'

Let us be contented during this generation with the assurance that geographically the Union has been preserved, and that each contending warrior has once more taken up the peaceful struggle for bettering and beautifying the home so bravely fought for.

CHAPTER XXX.

RECONSTRUCTION WITHOUT PAIN—ADMINISTRATIONS OF JOHNSON AND GRANT.

It was feared that the return of a million Federal soldiers to their homes after the four years of war would make serious trouble in the North, but they were very shortly adjusted to their new lives and attending to the duties which peace imposed upon them.

The war of the Rebellion was disastrous to nearly every branch of trade, but those who remained at home to write the war-songs of the North did well. Some of these efforts were worthy, and, buoyed up by a general feeling of robust patriotism, they floated on to success; but few have stood the test of years and monotonous peace. The author of 'Mother, I am hollow to the ground' is just depositing his profits from its sale in the picture given on next page. The second one, wearing the cape-overcoat tragedy air, wrote 'Who will be my laundress now?'

Andrew Johnson succeeded to Mr. Lincoln's seat, having acted before as his vice.

A great review of the army, lasting twelve hours, was arranged to take place in Washington, consisting of the armies of Grant and Sherman. It was reviewed by the President and Cabinet; it extended over thirty miles twenty men deep, and constituted about one-fifth of the Northern army at the time peace was declared.

President Johnson recognized the State governments existing in Virginia, Tennessee, Arkansas, and Louisiana, but instituted provisional governments for the other States of the defeated Confederacy, as it seemed impossible otherwise to bring order out of the chaos which war and financial distress had brought about. He authorized the assembly also of loyal conventions to elect State and other officers, and pardoned by proclamation everybody, with the exception of a certain class of the late insurgents whom he pardoned personally.

THE STAY-AT-HOMES WHO WROTE WAR-SONGS.

On Christmas Day, 1868, a Universal Amnesty was declared. The Thirteenth Amendment, abolishing slavery, became a part of the Constitution, December 18, 1865, and the former masters found themselves still morally responsible for these colored people, without the right to control them or even the money with which to employ them.

The annual interest on the national debt at this time amounted to one hundred and fifty million dollars. Yet the Treasury paid this, together with the expenses of government, and reduced the debt seventy-one million dollars before the volunteer army had been fully discharged in 1866.

Comment on such recuperative power as that is unnecessary; for the generation that fights a four-years war costing over two billions of dollars generally leaves the debt for another generation or another century to pay.

Congress met finally, ignored the President's rollicking welcome to the seceded States, and over his veto proceeded to pass various laws regarding their admission, such as the Civil Rights and Freedman's Bureau Bills.

Tennessee returned promptly to the Union under the Constitutional Amendments, but the others did not till the nightmare of Reconstruction had been added to the horrors of war. In 1868, after much time worse than wasted in carpet-bag government and a mob reign in the South which imperilled her welfare for many years after it was over, by frightening investors and settlers long after peace had been restored, representatives began to come into Congress under the laws.

During this same year the hostilities between Congress and the President culminated in an effort to impeach the latter. He escaped by one vote.

It is very likely that the assassination of Lincoln was the most unfortunate thing that happened to the Southern States. While he was not a warrior, he was a statesman, and no gentler hand or more willing brain could have entered with enthusiasm into the adjustment of chaotic conditions, than his.

The Fourteenth Amendment, a bright little *bon mot*, became a law June 28, 1868, and was written in the minutes of Congress, so that people could go there and refresh their memories regarding it. It guaranteed civil rights to all, regardless of race, color, odor, wildness or wooliness whatsoever, and allows all noses to be counted in Congressional representations, no matter what angle they may be at or what the color may be.

Some American citizens murmur at taxation without representation, but the negro murmurs at representation without remuneration.

The Fenian excitement of 1866 died out without much loss of life.

In October, 1867, Alaska was purchased from Russia for seven million two hundred thousand dollars. The ice-crop since then would more than pay for the place, and it has also a water-power and cranberry marsh on it.

The rule of the Imperialists in France prompted the appointment of Maximilian, Archduke of Austria, as Emperor of Mexico, supported by the French army. The Americans, still sore and in debt at the heels of their own war, pitied the helpless Mexicans, and, acting on the principles enunciated in the Monroe Doctrine, demanded the recall of Maximilian, who, deserted finally by his foreign abettors, was defeated and as a prisoner shot by the Mexicans, June 19, 1867.

The Atlantic cable was laid from Valentia Bay in Ireland to Heart's Content, Newfoundland, one thousand eight hundred and sixty-four miles, and the line from New York to the latter place built in 1856, a distance of one thousand miles, making in all, as keen mathematicians will see, two thousand eight hundred and sixty-four miles.

A very agreeable commercial treaty with China was arranged in 1868.

Grant and Colfax, Republicans, succeeded Andrew Johnson in the next election, Horatio Seymour, of New York, and Frank P. Blair, of Missouri, being the Democratic nominees. Virginia and Mississippi had not been fully reconstructed, and so were not yet permitted to vote. They have squared the matter up since, however, by voting with great enthusiasm.

In 1869 the Pacific Railroad was completed, whereby the trip from the Atlantic to the Pacific—three thousand and three hundred miles—might be made in a week. It also attracted the Asiatic trade, and tea, silk, spices, and leprosy found a new market in the land of the free and the home of the brave.

Still flushed with its success in humorous legislation, Congress, on the 30th of March, 1870, passed the Fifteenth Amendment, giving to the colored men the right to vote. It then became a part of the Constitution, and people who have seen it there speak very highly of it.

Prosperity now attracted no attention whatever. Gold, worth nearly three dollars at the close of the war, fell to a dollar and ten cents, and the debt during the first two years of this administration was reduced two hundred million dollars.

Genuine peace reigned in the entire Republic, and o'er the scarred and shell-torn fields of the South there waved, in place of hostile banners, once more the cotton and the corn. The red foliage of the gum-tree with the white in the snowy white cotton-fields and the blue-grass of Kentucky (blue-grass is not, strictly speaking, blue enough to figure in the national colors, but the author has taken out a poetic license which does not expire for over a year yet, and he therefore under its permission is allowed a certain amount of idiocy) showed that the fields had never forgotten their loyalty to the national colors. Peace under greatly changed conditions resumed her vocations, and, in the language of the poet, —

'There were domes of white blossoms where swelled the white tent; There were ploughs in the track where the war-wagons went; There were songs where they lifted up Rachel's lament.'

October 8, 1871, occurred the great fire in Chicago, raging for forty-eight hours and devastating three thousand acres of the city. Twenty-five thousand buildings were burned, and two hundred million dollars' worth of property. One hundred thousand people lost their houses, and over seven and one-half millions of dollars were raised for those who needed it, all parts of the world uniting to improve the joyful opportunity to do good, without a doubt of its hearty appreciation.

Boston also had a seventy-million dollar fire in the heart of the wholesale trade, covering sixty acres; and in the prairie and woods fires of Wisconsin, Minnesota, and Michigan, many people lost not only their homes but their lives. Fifteen hundred people perished in Wisconsin alone.

In 1871 the damage done by the Alabama, a British-built ship, and several other cruisers sent out partly to facilitate the cotton trade and partly to do a little fighting when a Federal vessel came that way, was assessed at fifteen million five hundred thousand dollars against Great Britain by the arbitrators who met at Geneva, Switzerland, and the northwestern boundary line between the United States and British America was settled by arbitration, the Emperor of Germany acting as arbitrator and deciding in favor of America.

This showed that people who have just wound up a big war have often learned some valuable sense; not two billion dollars' worth, perhaps, but some.

San Domingo was reported for sale, and a committee looked at it, priced it, etc., but Congress decided not to buy it.

The Liberal Republican party, or that element of the original party which was opposed to the administration, nominated Horace Greeley, of New York, while the old party renominated General Grant for the term to succeed himself. The latter was elected, and Mr. Greeley did not long survive his defeat.

The Modoc Indians broke loose in the early part of Grant's second term, and, leaping from their lava-beds early in the morning, Shacknasty Jim and other unlaundried children of the forest raised merry future punishment, and the government, always kind, always loving and sweet toward the red brother, sent a peace commission with popcorn balls and a gentle-voiced parson to tell Shacknasty James and Old Stand-up-and-Sit-down that the white father at Washington loved them and wanted them all to come and spend the summer at his house, and also that by sin death came into the world, and that we were all primordial germs at first, and that we should look up, not down, look out, not in, look forward, not backward, and lend a hand.

PEACE COMMISSION POW-WOWING WITH THE MODOCS.

It was at this moment that Early-to-Bed-and Early-to-Rise-Black Hawk and Shacknasty James, thinking that this thing had gone far enough, killed General Canby and wounded both Mr. Meacham and

Rev. Dr. Thomas, who had never had an unkind thought toward the Modocs in their lives.

The troops then allowed their ill temper to get the best of them, and asked the Modocs if they meant anything personal by their action, and, learning that they did, the soldiers did what with the proper authority they would have done at first, bombarded the children of the forest and mussed up their lava-beds so that they were glad to surrender.

In 1873 a panic occurred after the failure of Jay Cooke & Co., of Philadelphia, and a money stringency followed, the Democrats attributing it a good deal to the party in power, just as cheap Republicans twenty years later charged the Democratic administration with this same thing. Inconsistency of this kind keeps good men, like the writer, out of politics, and turns their attention toward the contemplation of a better land.

TALKING ABOUT THE CENTENNIAL.

In 1875 Centennial Anniversaries began to ripen and continued to fall off the different branches of government, according to the history of events so graphically set forth in the preceding pages. They were duly celebrated by a happy and self-made people. The Centennial Exposition at Philadelphia in 1876 was a marked success in every way, nearly ten millions of people having visited it, who claimed that it was well worth the price of admission.

Aside from the fact that these ten millions of people had talked about it to millions of folks at home,—or thought they had,—the Exposition was a boon to every one, and thousands of Americans went home with a knowledge of their country that they had never had before, and pointers on blowing out gas which saved many lives in after-years.

MOVE ON, MAROON BROTHER, MOVE ON!

CHAPTER XXXI.

CLOSING CHRONICLES.

In 1876 the peaceful Sioux took an outing, having refused to go to their reservation in accordance with the treaty made with the Great Father at Washington, D. C., and regular troops were sent against them.

General Custer, with the 7th Regiment, led the advance, and General Terry aimed for the rear of the children of the forest up the Big Horn. Here, on the 25th of June, without assistance, and with characteristic courage, General Custer attacked the enemy, sending Colonel Reno to fall on the rear of the village.

Scarcely enough of Custer's own command with him at the time lived long enough to tell the story of the battle. General Custer, his two brothers, and his nephew were among the dead. Reno held his ground until reinforced, but Custer's troops were exterminated.

It is said that the Sioux rose from the ground like bunch-grass and swarmed up the little hill like a pest of grasshoppers, mowing down the soldiers with the very newest and best weapons of warfare, and leaving nothing at last but the robbed and mutilated bodies lying naked in the desolate land of the Dakotah.

The Fenimore Cooper Indian is no doubt a brave and highly intellectual person, educated abroad, refined and cultivated by foreign travel, graceful in the grub dance or scalp walk-around, yet tender-hearted as a girl, walking by night fifty-seven miles in a single evening to warn his white friends of danger. The Indian introduced into literature was a bronze Apollo who bathed almost constantly and only killed white people who were unpleasant and coarse. He dressed in new and fresh buckskins, with trimming of same, and his sable hair hung glossy and beautiful down the coppery billows of muscles on his back.

The real Indian has the dead and unkempt hair of a busted buggy-cushion filled with hen feathers. He lies, he steals, he assassinates, he mutilates, he tortures. He needs Persian powder long before he needs the theology which abler men cannot agree upon. We can, in fact, only retain him as we do the buffalo, so long as he complies with the statutes. But the red brother is on his way to join the cave-bear, the three-toed horse, and the ichthyosaurus in the great fossil realm of the historic past. Move on, maroon brother, move on!

ON HIS WAY TO JOIN THE CAVE-BEAR, THE THREE-TOED
HORSE, AND THE ICHTHYOSAURUS.

Rutherford B. Hayes and William A. Wheeler were nominated in the
summer of 1876, and so close was the fight against Samuel J. Tilden
and Thomas A. Hendricks that friends of the latter to this day refer
to the selection of Hayes and Wheeler by a joint Electoral
Commission to whom the contested election was referred, as a fraud
and larceny on the part of the Republican party. It is not the part of
an historian, who is absolutely destitute of political principles, to
pass judgment. Facts have crept into this history, it is true, but no
one could regret it more than the author; yet there has been no bias
or political prejudice shown, other than that reflected from the
historical sources whence information was necessarily obtained.

Hayes was chosen, and gave the country an unruffled, unbiased
administration, devoid of frills, and absolutely free from the
appearance of hostility to any one. He was one of the most
conciliatory Presidents ever elected by Republican votes or counted
in by a joint Electoral Commission.

He withdrew all troops from the South, and in several Southern States things wore a Democratic air at once.

In 1873 Congress demonetized silver, and quite a number of business-men were demonetized at the same time; so in 1878 silver was made a legal tender for all debts. As a result, in 1879 gold for the first time in seventeen years sold at par.

Troubles arose in 1878 over the right to fish in the northeast waters, and the treaty at Washington resulted in an award to Great Britain of five million five hundred thousand dollars, with the understanding that wasteful fishing should cease, and that as soon as either party got enough for a mess he should go home, no matter how well the fish seemed to be biting.

The right to regulate Chinese immigration was given by treaty at Pekin, and ever since the Chinaman has entered our enclosures in some mysterious way, made enough in a few years to live like a potentate in China, and returned, leaving behind a pleasant memory and a chiffonnier here and there throughout the country filled with scorched shirt-bosoms, acid-eaten collars, and white vests with burglar-proof, ingrowing pockets in them.

The next nominations for President and Vice-President were James A. Garfield, of Ohio, and Chester A. Arthur, of New York, on the Republican ticket, and Winfield S. Hancock, of Pennsylvania, and William H. English, of Indiana, on the Democratic ticket. James B. Weaver was connected with this campaign also. Who will tell us what he had to do with it? Can no one tell us what James B. Weaver had to do with the campaign of 1881? Very well; I will tell you what he had to do with the campaign of 1881.

He was the Presidential candidate on the Greenback ticket, but it was kept so quiet that I am not surprised to know that you did not hear about it.

A PERSON JUMPING FROM IT IS NOT ALWAYS KILLED.

After the inauguration of Garfield the investigation and annulling of star-route contracts fraudulently obtained were carried out, whereby two million dollars' worth of these corrupt agreements were rendered null and void.

On the morning of July 2, President Garfield was shot by a poor, miserable, unbalanced, and abnormal growth whose name will not be discovered even in the appendix of this work. He was tried, convicted, and sent squealing into eternity.

The President lingered patiently for two months and a half, when he died.

After the accession of President Arthur, there occurred floods on the lower Mississippi, whereby one hundred thousand people lost their homes. The administration was not in any way to blame for this.

In 1883 the Brooklyn Bridge across East River was completed and ready for jumping purposes. It was regarded as a great engineering success at the time, but it is now admitted that it is not high enough. A person jumping from it is not always killed.

The same year the Civil Service Bill became a law. It provides that competitive examinations shall be made of certain applicants for office, whereby mail-carriers must prove that they know how to teach school, and guards in United States penitentiaries are required to describe how to navigate a ship.

Possibly recent improvements have been made by which the curriculum is more fitted to the crime, but in the early operations of the law the janitor of a jail had to know what length shadow would be cast by a pole 18 feet 6¼ inches high on the third day of July at 11 o'clock 30 min. and 20 sec. standing on a knoll 35 feet 8⅛ inches high, provided 8 men in 9 days can erect such a pole working 8 hours per day.

In 1883 letter postage was reduced from three cents to two cents per half-ounce, and in 1885 to two cents per ounce.

In 1884 Alaska was organized as a Territory, and after digging the snow out of Sitka, so that the governor should not take cold in his system, it was made the seat of government.

Chinese immigration in 1882 was forbidden for ten years, and in 1884 a treaty with Mexico was made, a copy of which is on file in the State Department, but not allowed to be loaned to the author for use in this work.

Grover Cleveland and Thomas A. Hendricks were nominated and elected at the end of President Arthur's term, running against James G. Blaine and John A. Logan, the Republican candidates, also Benjamin F. Butler and A. M. West, of Mississippi, on the People's ticket, and John P. St. John and William Daniel on the Prohibition ticket. St. John went home and kept bees, so that he could have honey to eat on his Kansas locusts, and Daniel swore he would never enter the performing cage of immoral political wild beasts again while reason remained on her throne.

In 1886 a Presidential succession law was passed, whereby on the death of the President and the Vice-President the order of succession shall be the Secretary of State, the Secretary of the Treasury, the Secretary of War, the Attorney-General, the Postmaster-General, and the Secretaries of the Navy and of the Interior. This gives the Secretary of Agriculture an extremely remote and rarefied chance at the Presidency. Still, he should be just as faithful to his trust as he would be if he were nearer the throne.

May 4, 1886, occurred a terrible outbreak of Chicago Anarchists, whereby seven policemen sent to preserve order were killed by the bursting of an Anarchist's bomb. The Anarchists were tried and executed, with the exception of Ling, who ate a dynamite capsule and passed into rest having had his features, and especially his nose, blown in a swift and earnest manner. Death resulted, and whiskers and beer-blossoms are still found embedded in the stone walls of his cell. Those who attended the funeral say that Ling from a scenic point of view was not a success.

Governor Altgeld, of Illinois, an amateur American, in the summer of 1893 pardoned two of the Anarchists who had escaped death by imprisonment.

August 31, 1886, in Charleston, occurred several terrible earthquake shocks, which seriously damaged the city and shocked and impaired the nerves and health of hundreds of people.

The noted heroism and pluck of the people of Charleston were never shown to greater advantage than on this occasion.

Mr. Cleveland was again nominated, but was defeated by General Benjamin Harrison. Hon. James G. Blaine, of Maine, was made Secretary of State, and Wm. Windom, a veteran financier, Secretary of the Treasury. Secretary Windom's tragic death just as he had finished a most brilliant address to the great capitalists of New York after their annual dinner and discussion at Delmonico's is, and will ever remain, while life lasts, a most dramatic picture in the author's memory.

Personally, the administration of President Harrison will be long remembered for the number of deaths among the families of the Executive and those of his Cabinet and friends.

Nebraska, the thirty-seventh State, was admitted March 1, 1867. The name signifies 'Water Valley.' Colorado, the Centennial State, was the thirty-eighth. She was admitted July 1, 1876. Six other States have been since admitted when the political sign was right. Still, they have not always stuck by the party admitting them to the Union. This is the kind of ingratitude which sometimes leads to the reformation of politicians supposed to have been dead in sin.

President Harrison's administration was a thoroughly upright and honest one, so far as it was possible for it to be after his party had drifted into the musty catacombs of security in office and the ship of state had become covered with large and expensive barnacles.

As we go to press, his successor, Grover Cleveland, in the first year of his second administration, is paying a high price for fleeting fame, with the serious question of what to do with the relative coinage of gold and silver, and the Democrats in Congress, for the first time in the history of the world, are referring each other with hot breath and flashing eye to the platform they adopted at the National Convention.

Heretofore among the politicians a platform, like that on the railway cars, 'is made for the purpose of helping the party to get aboard, but not to ride on.'

The Columbian Exposition and World's Fair at Chicago in the summer of 1893 eclipsed all former Exhibitions, costing more and showing greater artistic taste, especially in its buildings, than anything preceding it. Some gentle warfare resulted from a struggle over the question of opening the 'White City' on Sunday, and a great deal of bitterness was shown by those who opposed the opening and who had for years favored the Sunday closing of Niagara. A doubtful victory was obtained by the Sunday openers, for so many of the exhibitors closed their departments that visitors did not attend on Sunday in paying quantities.

Against a thousand odds and over a thousand obstacles, especially the apprehension of Asiatic cholera and the actual sudden appearance of a gigantic money panic, Chicago, heroic and victorious, carried out her mighty plans and gave to the world an exhibition that won golden opinions from her friends and stilled in dumb wonder the jealousy of her enemies.

In the mean time, the author begs leave to thank his readers for the rapt attention shown in perusing these earnest pages, and to apologize for the tears of sympathy thoughtlessly wrung from eyes unused to weep, by the graphic word-painting and fine education shown by the author.

It was not the intention of the writer to touch the fountain of tears and create wash-outs everywhere, but sometimes tears do one good.

In closing, would it be out of place to say that the stringency of the money market is most noticeable and most painful, and for that reason would it be too much trouble for the owner of this book to refuse to loan it, thereby encouraging its sale and contributing to the comfort of a deserving young man?

THE END.

APPENDIX.

The idea of an appendix to this work was suggested by a relative, who promised to prepare it, but who has been detained now for over a year in one of the public buildings of Colorado on the trumped-up charge of horse-stealing. The very fact that he was not at once hanged shows that the charge was not fully sustained, and that the horse was very likely of little value.

THE AUTHOR.

FOOTNOTES

[1] The author acknowledges especially the courtesy of San Diego Colon Columbus, a son of the great navigator, whose book 'Historiadores Primitivos' was so generously loaned the author by relatives of young Columbus.

I have refrained from announcing in the foregoing chapter the death of Columbus, which occurred May 20, 1506, at Valladolid, the funeral taking place from his late residence, because I dislike to give needless pain.

B. N

[2] See Dr. Dunn's Family Physician and Horse Doctor.

[3] This is a stanza from the works of Dempster Winterbottom Woodworth, M.D., of Ellsworth, Pierce County, Wisconsin, author of the 'Diary of Judge Pierce,' and 'Life and Times of Melancthon Klingensmith.' The thanks of the author are also due to Baldy Sowers for a loaned copy of 'How to Keep up a Pleasing Correspondence without Conveying Information,' 8vo, bevelled boards, published by Public Printer.

[4] The authority given for this statement, I admit, is meagre, but it is as accurate as many of the figures by means of which people prove things. — B. N.

[5] While the Union forces did not succeed in beating Stonewall Jackson back, in returning to Washington they succeeded in beating everybody else back. (See Appendix.)

[6] The odium to be cast on the person upon whom it should fall for the sickening defeat at Bull Run was found to be in such wretched condition at the time these lines were written that it was decided to go on without casting it. The writer points with pride to the fact that in writing this history fifteen cents' worth of odium will cover the entire amount used.

Printed in the United States
98921LV00002B/31/A

9 781406 549737